I0813995

# THE STORY OF
# ASTON MARTIN

First published in 2024 by Welbeck
An imprint of Headline Publishing Group Limited

4



Cataloguing in Publication Data is available from the British Library

ISBN 9781802798487

Printed and bound in Italy

Headline's policy is to use papers that are natural, renewable and recyclable products and made from wood grown in well-managed forests and other controlled sources. The logging and manufacturing processes are expected to conform to the environmental regulations of the country of origin.



Editor: Conor Kilgallon
Design: Rebecca Hills & Luana Gobbo
Production: Rachel Burgess

HEADLINE PUBLISHING GROUP LIMITED
A Hachette UK Company
Carmelite House
50 Victoria Embankment
London EC4Y 0DZ

The authorised representative in the EEA is Hachette Ireland,
8 Castlecourt Centre, Dublin 15, D15 XTP3, Ireland (email: info@hbgi.ie)

www.headline.co.uk
www.hachette.co.uk

# THE STORY OF ASTON MARTIN

A TRIBUTE TO
AUTOMOTIVE EXCELLENCE

PETER TOMALIN

ASTON MARTIN

# CONTENTS

# IN THE
# BEGINNING

# BAMFORD & MARTIN

A fledgling company founded by two visionary motoring enthusiasts; cars built in tiny numbers; a reputation forged in motorsport; and perpetually precarious finances leading to several changes of ownership – these were the hallmarks of Aston Martin's formative years.

Ironically, it was a shared love of cycling that brought together the two young Englishmen who would create the very first Aston Martins. While bonding over pedal power, Old Etonian Lionel Martin and his cycling club chum, Robert Bamford, quickly discovered that they also shared a passion for four-wheeled transport; on 15 January 1913 they founded Bamford & Martin Ltd "*to deal in, manufacture and sell motor cars*", all from a small workshop in Henniker Mews, Kensington.

Bamford, the Essex-born son of a curate, was a trained engineer, but it was Lionel who was the real driving force (quite often literally) of the fledgling company. Born on 15 March 1878 into a wealthy family of Cornish china clay merchants, Lionel was 13 when he entered Eton College, where he first developed his keen interest in competitive

OPPOSITE: Founders Lionel Martin (left) and Robert Bamford.

cycling. In 1902, with a BA from Oxford, he moved to London, where he became a member of the prestigious Bath Road (cycling) Club. He went on to hold several records on bicycles and tricycles, most notably the Land's End to London tricycle record in a remarkable 22 hours, 16 minutes and 16 seconds – especially remarkable when you consider it snowed! It was through the club that he was to meet Robert Bamford.

The incorporation of Bamford & Martin in January 1913 was, of course, just a business formality – the really interesting stuff was about to start. Initially, they specialized in the tuning of 10hp Singers, but later that year they began work on a car of their own, fired with the ambition to make a "*British-built fast touring car… built up to the high ideals demanded by a small but extremely discriminating class of motorist*".

Martin, the more accomplished driver of the two and a regular competitor in races and hillclimbs, was soon regularly out testing the first prototype, often referred to as 'the hybrid', because while the engine was new, the chassis came from a 1908 Isotta Fraschini.

The name they had coined for their car was Aston-Martin, the 'Aston' part being the brainwave of Lionel's wife, Kate Martin, following Lionel's early competition successes on the Aston Hillclimb in Buckinghamshire, the masterstroke being that it would mean their cars would often appear first in any alphabetical listings.

An article in *The Light Car and Cyclecar* dated 19 October 1913 carried the headline "*Mr Lionel Martin to Produce a Light Car*". The accompanying story ran:

> *"His idea is to produce something which is a really high-class vehicle of a semi-sporting character. With his great experience of trials, such qualities as speed, stability, reliability and hill-climbing should predominate.*

*"The component factors of the car, which is to be known as the Aston-Martin, are being made by the best works in the country, and although the machine will not be ready for several months, Mr Martin is at present testing out the engine, which has been specially made for him by the Coventry-Simplex people...*

*"We were recently privileged to accompany him on one of his 100-mile high-speed test runs. The engine, which is about 1400cc, is at present fitted in a comparatively heavy and old type of Italian racing car, which pulls along the road in a really extremely vivacious manner."*

BELOW: The car known as 'the hybrid', which featured a 1.4-litre engine specially made for Bamford & Martin, tackles the Cindertrack Hill in Brighton, October 1914.

Among these test runs, Lionel joined a small group of other pioneering motorists on Sunday, 25 October 1914, and set out from London for Brighton in the hybrid car, accompanied by a journalist and a photographer from *The Light Car and Cyclecar*.

What the unnamed photographer captured that day were the first known photographs of a car powered by Bamford & Martin's own engine as it took on the local Cindertrack Hill. In fact, 'the hybrid' made several successful ascents of the 1-in-3 climb, each time Martin inviting another of his pioneering chums to climb on board. The point had been made.

In 1915, Bamford & Martin foreman Jack Addis and fitter Frank Hunt assembled the first true Aston-Martin, registered on 16 March, its upswept cowl earning it the irreverent nickname 'Coal Scuttle'. But the progress of the fledgling car company would soon be put on hold as war intensified in Europe. The small workshops in Henneker Mews closed; the machinery went to the Sopwith Aviation Company. Martin joined the Admiralty, Bamford the Royal Army Service Corps.

But even while the workshops were mothballed, Lionel would find time to test 'Coal Scuttle'. When it reappeared at the gruelling 400-mile (644km) London to Edinburgh Trial in June 1919 after Martin had reassembled his little team at Henniker Mews, it had some 15,000 miles (24,140km) on the clock! The trial was Aston-Martin's first ever competitive event, driver Jack Addis winning a gold medal for completing it on time.

RIGHT: The very first Aston-Martin (the name was hyphenated in the early days) known as 'Coal Scuttle', with Lionel's wife, 'Calamity Kate' Martin, at the wheel.

ABOVE: Lionel Martin (on the left) at Brooklands in 1921 with the second Aston-Martin, nicknamed 'Bunny', which saw Aston-Martin's international debut later that year.

In January 1920, Bamford & Martin moved to larger premises at 53, Abingdon Road, off Kensington High Street, and in April 'Coal Scuttle' was entered in the London to Land's End Trial, this time with Lionel at the wheel. Again, they came back with a gold medal.

Finances were always tight, though. Robert Bamford soon left the scene and Lionel began to sell off his inheritance from one family business, realizing what at the time was an enormous sum – £24,445 (£1.3 million in today's money) – which he began to pour into the construction and running of the cars.

Aston-Martin's debut at Brooklands followed in May 1921, Lionel winning the first race of the day, and later that year the marque made its international debut in the Voiturette Grand Prix at Le Mans (not the 24 Hours, which came later). Its second car, known as 'Bunny', led the race in the early stages before dropping back to finish a creditable sixth against strong opposition.

ABOVE: Mud, glorious mud! Lionel and co-driver Kate Martin tackling a typically challenging road on the gruelling London to Land's End Trial in March 1921.

These early Aston Martins often tended to have pet names, usually coined by 'Calamity Kate' Martin. Car number three was painted black, and its original name would appall modern sensibilities. Today it is the oldest surviving Aston Martin, but is now known by its chassis number – A3.

Power came from a sidevalve 1487cc four-cylinder of broadly Bamford & Martin's own creation but with some parts made by Coventry-Simplex. At Brooklands in 1921, A3 wore a new (and temporary) streamlined long-tail body as it took several light-car speed records – including 100 miles at an average of 86.2mph (160km at an average of 138.7km/h).

The marque was attracting the interest of a number of rich playboys, among them the racer Count Zborowski, who invested £10,270 (more than £650,000 in today's money), enabling the firm to enter two cars in the 1922 French Grand Prix, though neither finished. Record-breaker Captain George Eyston also bought two works racers while a single-seater,

'Razor Blade', named for its unfeasibly small frontal area which allowed a top speed of around 100mph (160km/h), was built to attack Brooklands speed records.

Despite all this success – and fresh investment from another enthusiastic upper-class benefactor, Lady Charnwood – sales to the general public were slow, and the cash-strapped company was wound up in June 1926 after the production of just 63 cars.

Lionel Martin departed amid bitter recriminations, but for him there was a happy ending. In 1929, a further inheritance gave him financial security and he remained active in the motoring and cycling worlds, eventually passing away in October 1945 at the age of 67, a week after he had been in collision with a car while on his tricycle.

BELOW: On the left, the oldest surviving Aston, known as A3, with the single-seater 'Razor Blade', built to break speed records on the Brooklands banking.

XR 1981

There would be a happy ending for the marque he created too, for later in 1926 it was resurrected, now as Aston Martin Motors Ltd (no hyphen) under one Domenico Augustus Cesare Bertelli. Or 'Bert' Bertelli, as he was known to everyone.

Bertelli, despite his impressively Italian name, was in fact an honorary Brit. An honorary Welshman, to be more accurate, because his family moved to Cardiff in 1894, four years after his birth in Italy.

From school he moved on to the local steelworks, where an aptitude for engineering led him to the pattern and tool shops. It took a return to Italy, however, to fire up interest in the new world of motor cars. While working for Fiat, he rode as Felice Nazzaro's mechanic in the 1908 Targa Bologna, which they won.

Back in Britain in the 1920s, Bert continued to race, becoming well known at Brooklands for his dashing manner and chain-smoking habit. He also teamed up with fellow engineer William 'Bill' Renwick to form Renwick & Bertelli, or R&B, with plans to create their own high-class touring car. For this they developed a new engine – a 1.5-litre, overhead-camshaft 'four' – which they also planned to sell to other carmakers. But then the ailing Aston Martin enterprise became available and plans took a different course.

Bertelli knew Aston Martin's owners and was aware of their financial problems, and in October 1926 he and Bill Renwick bought the old company for £10,000. Now their vision of an upmarket tourer could wear a badge with established prestige. It was the opening of a brand-new chapter in a back-from-the-brink history that would have a habit of repeating itself.

With finance from John Benson (later to become Lord Charnwood), they set up Aston Martin Motors in the former Whitehead Aircraft factory at Feltham, Middlesex. Bert Bertelli's brother Enrico, known more anglophilically as Harry,

OPPOSITE: One of the very earliest Aston-Martin road cars, 'Cloverleaf', pictured on Aston Hill, Buckinghamshire, scene of some of Lionel Martin's early successes.

had meanwhile developed a business building stylish, high-quality bodywork, and he too set up a workshop nearby to clothe his brother's products. Aston Martin's Bertelli era was underway.

The new 1492cc OHC engine would power the 'First Series' range (interestingly all pre-war Astons had four-cylinder engines, with the vast majority being 1.5 litres), and business went well at first, but by 1929 Renwick and Benson had fallen out with each other and both had left the company. That left Bert Bertelli, supported by a succession of wealthy backers, in sole charge of engineering and racing activity. And

through these turbulent times, there was plenty of the latter. Bertelli himself raced at Le Mans in 1928, when the company entered its first dedicated Le Mans cars, LM1 and LM2. Both retired, but the example Bertelli shared with George Eyston was running seventh when it stopped after 350 miles (565km), and Aston Martin won a special prize for fastest 1.5-litre car over the first 20 laps. More prizes would follow, both at home and abroad, and in 1930, partly driven by this on-track success, car production reached a record 68 units.

It was a false dawn. The following year just 32 cars were built for sale and in 1932 the number dropped again to 27.

BELOW: By the early '30s, with Aston Martin now under the direction of 'Bert' Bertelli, the range included handsome, low-slung, sporting machines like this 'Le Mans'.

Body mounting.

To the rescue this time came Newcastle ship-owner and philanthropist Sir Arthur Sutherland, who bought Aston Martin for £10,000 in 1933, his son Gordon becoming joint managing director with Bert Bertelli. A wider sales network and better management saw production rise dramatically to 106 cars.

An improved 'Mark II' was introduced for 1934, a year that again saw annual production top 100 cars. Meanwhile a three-car entry won the team prize in the prestigious Ulster Tourist Trophy, leading to the introduction of the stylish 'Ulster' two-seater road-racer – the most coveted of all pre-war Astons.

By the mid-1930s, Aston Martin's reputation was on a high, but so were tensions within the company. The financial men wanted to broaden the range and increase sales with a more docile road car, but Bertelli considered this a sell-out.

BELOW: The best-known Aston dating from before WWII was the brilliant 'Ulster', so named after a successful outing for the factory team in the Ulster Tourist Trophy.

OPPOSITE: The MkII model in production at Victoria Road, Feltham, circa 1935. Sporting, tourer and saloon variants were also offered.

ABOVE: With the Aston 'wings' now very much in evidence, this early '30s brochure was as stylish as the cars it represented; Aston Martin was clearly aiming for the smart set.

They also stopped buying bodies from Harry Bertelli, which was clearly awkward. In February 1937, Bert left, suddenly and completely, not just Aston Martin but the entire motor industry. His place as the engineering force behind Aston Martin was taken by Claude Hill, his right-hand man since the Renwick & Bertelli days.

New models were introduced, but in 1938 production fell to just 14 units and in 1939 a mere six cars were sold as storm clouds gathered over Europe once again. There was, however, one glimmer of hope for the marque. In March 1939, Aston Martin patented its "car of the future", designed by Hill. Christened 'Atom', the prototype was completed early in

1940. One of the first fully functional 'concept cars' ever built, it explored a number of new technologies and focused on low weight and a rigid structure. Featuring a 2-litre engine, it did away with the traditional body-on-frame construction, using rectangular cross-section steel tubing for both the main chassis and the support framework for the streamlined aluminium body. Among its other innovations, it was also the first Aston with independent front suspension – and would yet have a critical part to play in the story of Aston Martin.

BELOW: It had slightly odd proportions and would remain a one-off, but the 1940 'Atom' was an important car in the Aston Martin story, as time would tell.

# THE
# 'DB' ERA

# THE NAME'S BROWN...

After the struggles of the interwar years, a period of prosperity was about to dawn. Led by the industrialist David Brown, who had ambitions to take on the likes of Ferrari, both in the showroom and on the racetrack, Aston Martin was about to enter its first golden age.

Aston Martin survived the war on military contracts, while managing director Gordon Sutherland clocked up an astonishing 100,000 miles (160,000km) in 'Atom'. However, lacking the means to develop an entirely new model, he placed a classified advertisement in *The Times* in 1946, offering for sale a "*High Class Motor Business*". That advertisement was spotted by a northern industrialist with a penchant for fast cars, field sports and pretty women. His name, David Brown.

Brown's grandfather (also called David) had established what became a hugely successful gear-making firm, David Brown & Sons, headquartered in Huddersfield, Yorkshire. Born in 1904, the young David was steeped in the family business – and in speed – from an early age. When he finished his grammar school education, he entered the business at the

OPPOSITE: A keen huntsman, David Brown enjoyed both kinds of horsepower.

age of 17 as an engineering apprentice, while spending his spare time riding, tuning and racing motorcycles – until his father forebade him from racing. And after the bikes came cars, as he built a number of 'specials' and competed in hillclimbs with considerable skill.

Then things got serious on the work front. In 1933, having had a thorough grounding in the David Brown company and not yet 30, he became managing director and was now head of an organization that at its height employed 17,000 people. Under his leadership the company expanded its activities significantly, including setting up in tractor manufacturing, but Brown's great love remained glamorous cars.

So Gordon Sutherland's advert naturally piqued his interest. On inquiring further, Brown discovered that the company was Aston Martin, and a few days later he visited the company's headquarters at Feltham and drove the Atom.

He was not taken with its 2-litre pushrod engine, but he was impressed by its handling and could see the potential in its underpinnings, as well as in the Aston Martin name. The asking price was £30,000 but, ever the deal-maker, Brown entered negotiations and in February 1947 bought a controlling stake in Aston Martin for £20,500 (a little over £1 million in today's money).

Work soon began on the first of a new generation of Aston Martins, using Atom's underpinnings but with Brown favouring an open body.

Construction of a prototype began in the hangars of the old Hanworth Air Park in Feltham, with engineering chief Claude Hill and ace driver Jock Horsfall in charge of development duties.

St John 'Jock' Horsfall was one of the more colourful characters in the Aston Martin story. A successful and talented racing driver in the 1930s, he was noticed by MI5, who used

him as a driver for covert ops during the war years, most famously in Operation Mincemeat, which laid a smokescreen for the Allied invasion of Italy in 1943.

Horsfall now persuaded Brown to let him enter the prototype 2-litre for the 1948 Spa 24-hour race – and won, earning the reborn Aston Martin company some welcome publicity. Later that year, now fitted with an elegant two-seater body by chief stylist Frank Feeley, the production model, the 2 Litre Sports, made its debut at the London motor show.

In the meantime, Brown had solved the longer-term need for a more powerful engine by acquiring the Lagonda company, complete with its W. O. Bentley-designed 2.6-litre 'LB6' twin-overhead-cam straight-six engine.

ABOVE: The 2-litre Sports model, retrospectively renamed DB1, was the first Aston road car of the DB era. It looked the part, but performance was modest.

ABOVE: The 1950 brochure for the DB2 cleverly positioned it with the then-new de Havilland Comet, the world's first commercial jet airliner. A new age had arrived.

All was not sweetness and light. Gordon Sutherland and Claude Hill, unhappy with the way the company was developing under Brown, left early in 1949; however, another fine engineer, Ted Cutting, joined from Allard later in the year. On the car front, the exciting news was the appearance of three 'DB2's with sleek Frank Feeley-designed coupé bodies at Le Mans, one of them with the new 2.6-litre Lagonda engine.

That car failed to finish, though a four-cylinder DB2 came seventh, but a new star had been born. The DB2 went into production in April 1950 with the Lagonda engine and a chassis strengthened by a Ted Cutting redesign, and it combined these assets to profound effect.

It was the first to wear the initials that would become every bit as revered by motoring enthusiasts as the Aston wings themselves. The DB2 also created the template for generations of Astons to come: a powerful, large-capacity engine under a rakishly long bonnet; sleek fastback bodywork with the option of a drophead version; a well-appointed cabin and, of course, excellent road manners.

The DB2 had a pretty handy competition record, too. When three cars were entered for the 1950 Le Mans, two of them finished first and second in the 3-litre class and fifth and sixth overall. The DB2, then, was every inch a sporting car, even if its performance figures – 0–60mph in 12.4s and a top speed of 116mph (187km/h) – do not sound fast today. A competition-spec 'Vantage' version, which lifted the output of the straight-six from 105 to 125bhp, chiefly courtesy of larger SU carburettors, was usefully quicker (0–60 in 10.7s, 117mph (188km/h) all-out).

Road testers of the day were in raptures about the new Aston Martin. The staff of *The Autocar* racked up a remarkable 1,900 miles (3,058km) in 10 days, describing the engine as "*one of the finest in existence*" and praising the DB2's high-speed stability.

BELOW: One of the three DB2s that competed at Le Mans in 1949, UMC 65 finished third in class and seventh overall. The following year DB2s would do even better.

BELOW: In the early '50s Astons were assembled at the David Brown works in Farsley, Yorkshire. On the line here are DB2/4s, distinguished by their hatchback tails.

A revised model, the DB2/4, arrived in 1953, reworked by Ted Cutting to add two occasional rear seats (hence the '4'), the backs of which could be folded forward to create a very useful load area that could be accessed via a handy, top-hinged tailgate – an innovation that gave the Aston reasonable claim to being the world's first 'hatchback'.

Engine capacity grew to 2.9 litres in 1954, peak power climbing to 140bhp, dropping the 0–60 time to 10.5s and lifting the maximum to a nice round 120mph (193km/h). For those in want of even more, Aston offered a Special Series engine with larger valves, higher-lift camshafts and a quoted 165bhp.

Meanwhile an all-new sports/racer, the DB3S, was scoring its first wins on track (see Chapter 7) and wowing everyone with its voluptuous lines – the work of Frank Feeley, the unsung design hero who also shaped all the early post-war Aston road cars.

At this time the road car chassis were being built alongside David Brown tractors at Farsley, near Huddersfield, and fitted with fully trimmed bodywork supplied by coachbuilders Mulliner. However, frustrated by Mulliner's inability to cope with DB2/4 body production, David Brown bought the historic Tickford coachworks at Newport Pagnell to make bodywork 'in house' and in 1955 chassis production also switched to the Buckinghamshire town.

By 1957 the new works was producing the DB MkIII, the final incarnation of the Claude Hill chassis and the Lagonda twin-cam six (now 3 litres and partially redesigned by Aston's new Polish-born chief engineer, Tadek Marek). The MkIII was also the company's first road car to feature what we now know as the 'classic' Aston grille. It was a fine car, but Aston Martin was about to step up to a whole new level.

ABOVE: Aston Martin hit a new high in 1958 with the launch of the DB4, and the following year with the short-wheelbase high-performance DB4 GT (pictured).

"*This is a very promising motor car*," David Brown is reported to have told chassis designer Harold Beach after his first drive in the DB4 in 1958. In October that year, the new model made its debut at the Paris motor show. It was one of those pivotal moments that happen only a handful of times in the story of a motor manufacturer, and nothing would ever be quite the same again.

There had been plenty of good-looking Astons before, from the pre-war Ulster to the DB MkIII. The DB4 brought something new. Unmistakably Aston Martin, but glamorous and sophisticated in a way no Aston had ever been before, it bestowed Ferrari/Maserati levels of desirability. That was no accident, of course, David Brown having turned to Italy to clothe the new engine and chassis.

The shape was credited to Touring of Milan – these were the days before car designers were openly feted, so the actual stylist, Federico Formenti, went unsung at the time – and the balance of proportions was perfection. The genius of the design was the way it blended Italian elegance with a kind of tailored, clipped Britishness.

Touring was also responsible for the method of construction, which again was new to Aston. Its patented Superleggera (super-light) system comprised a framework of small-diameter steel tubes attached to a sturdy steel platform and clothed in aluminium body panels. Touring licensed the system to Aston Martin, so that DB4s could be built in Newport Pagnell. The method gave a more rigid structure, to the benefit of performance and refinement. A welcome bonus was that it allowed a larger door aperture and lower sills, providing easier access to the sumptuously trimmed interior.

The other big news lay under the bonnet. Tadek Marek's all-new, 3.7-litre, all-Aston engine featured an aluminum cylinder block and crankcase topped by an aluminium cylinder head

with twin chain-driven overhead camshafts. With twin SU HD8 carburettors, it made a quoted 240bhp at 5,500rpm and drove through a four-speed David Brown gearbox. Top speed was dependent on the final drive, but in 1960 *Autocar* recorded 140mph (225km/h).

With the DB4, Aston Martin vaulted effortlessly into the top flight of the world's most desirable marques. And when the following summer the racing department and the fabulous DBR1 beat all comers at Le Mans and also carried off the World Sportscar Championship, Britain suddenly had its own Ferrari.

Ted Cutting and Harold Beach soon went to work on a racier DB4, too. The wheelbase was shortened. Out went the back seats and in went a 30-gallon fuel tank. Side and rear glass became Perspex and the headlights were streamlined

ABOVE: David Brown (with jacket and tie) celebrates winning the 1959 World Sportscar Championship with drivers Carroll Shelby, Stirling Moss, Roy Salvadori and Jack Fairman.

**1963 ASTON MARTIN DB4** No car is better suited to the individualist than the DB4 ; and this latest Saloon has new qualities that make it even more desirable.

A subtle change in styling gives a longer, sleeker line from end to end, and a much bigger boot. Comfort inside the car is increased by additional head-room at the back and infinitely adjustable front seats. The instrument layout has been re-arranged in detail and an oil thermometer added as standard equipment.

All these improvements add to the comfort and well-being of driver and passengers, and this extends to changes in the mechanical specification. The twin plate clutch combines high torque capacity with light pedal action. The steering ratio has been increased $12\frac{1}{2}\%$ and provides more effortless steering without loss of precision. An independent thermostatically controlled fan reduces noise in the car to a remarkable degree and also saves up to 7 h.p. at maximum speeds – which are in excess of 140 m.p.h.

under covers, providing a foretaste of how the DB5 would look. Under the bonnet was a twin-plug version of Tadek Marek's straight-six, with power up from 240 to 302bhp, slashing the 0–60mph time from around 8sec to a whisker over 6s, while the top speed rose from around 140 to a genuine 150mph (241km/h).

The DB4 GT was launched at the 1959 London motor show and something even more exotic was to come the following year, in the sublime shape of the DB4 GT Zagato – even lighter, even faster, even more beautiful. And one of the rarest and most prized of all Astons, with just 19 built in period.

Meanwhile, demand for the 'regular' DB4 greatly outstripped the ability to supply cars for several years and the model would evolve through five distinct series between 1958 and 1963. In fact it could well have entered a sixth series – but late in the day it was decided that the latest round of upgrades

ABOVE: The DB4 evolved constantly throughout its life; here is a brochure for the 1963 model, which boasted a bigger boot and additional headroom among other refinements.

OPPOSITE: Rarest and most desirable of all DB4 variants was the DB4 GT Zagato, with ultra-lightweight bodywork.

merited a new badge. And so was born the DB5. It featured a 4-litre straight-six engine in place of the outgoing DB4's 3.7-litre unit, with peak power up from 240 to 282bhp. Magazine road testers recorded 0–60mph times as low as 7 seconds and a top speed of around 142mph (229km/h), even more for the 'Vantage' version. It also introduced a five-speed gearbox (quite a novelty at the time) and dual-circuit Girling disc brakes with twin servos, while standard equipment now included Triplex 'Sundym' tinted glass and electric windows. The sports saloon was becoming a sophisticated GT car.

Early adopters included various Beatles and Rolling Stones. Oh, and a certain MI6 agent (more on which in Chapter 8). The motoring press loved it, too. "*The handling of the car is well up to its great accelerative powers*", declared *Autocar* in its September 1964 road test.

In fact the Most Famous Car in the World had only a short production run. In 1965 it was replaced, and where the '5 had been, in reality, little more than another evolution of the DB4, the DB6 was a genuinely new model. By adding almost 4in (10cm) to the wheelbase and raising the roofline over the rear seats, it was now a passable four-seater; it also featured a sharply abbreviated 'Kamm' tail with a built-in spoiler, shown by wind tunnel tests to reduce lift at the rear wheels by over 30 per cent. That it also gave a little more boot-space was a practical bonus.

Under the new skin, the basic structure and mechanical package were pretty much carried over from the DB5, with a Vantage version of the 4-litre straight-six available at no extra cost. With triple Webers and slightly racier cams, this gave 325bhp (up from the 314bhp of the DB5 Vantage). Aston claimed a top speed of over 150mph (241km/h), though only *Autocar*'s John Bolster achieved that (a two-way average of 152mph, 245km/h). Most magazines reckoned on a maximum of around 145mph (233km/h) with 0–60 in around 7 seconds

OPPOSITE: There are few finer sights in motoring than a DB4 GT in full flight. Among other things, it introduced the faired-in headlights that would be seen again on the DB5.

OVERLEAF: The twin peaks of the DB road car era, DB4 on the left, and DB5 on the right, the latter featuring a 4-litre straight-six where the '4' had a 3.7.

850 PPG

XXH 871

YJR 969

with the manual gearbox, an automatic now being another option for customers.

The DB6 was well received, but the designers and engineers at Newport Pagnell were already working on its intended replacement. The DBS, with its longer, wider chassis and all-new, razor-edged body designed by Aston's own William Towns, was launched in 1967. It had been conceived to run with a brand-new all-alloy 5.3-litre V8 engine designed by engineering maestro Tadek Marek, but teething problems with the new engine meant it had to be launched with the familiar 4-litre straight-six. It was, though, the first road-going Aston to replace the live rear axle with a more sophisticated de Dion rear end.

DB6 and DBS would in fact run in parallel for three years, and in 1969 the DB6 MkII and MkII Volante arrived with gently flared wheelarches to accommodate wider wheels and tyres (shared with the DBS). Power steering was now standard and there was the option of electronic fuel injection, a first on a British car.

BELOW: 1965 saw the launch of the DB6, with an extended roofline creating more space for rear passengers and a flipped-up 'Kamm' tail for improved high-speed stability.

ABOVE: The DBS, launched in 1967, brought sharper lines and, from 1969, the introduction of Aston Martin's fabulous all-aluminium quad-cam V8 engine.

The same year, Aston Martin got the royal seal of approval when the Queen gave Prince Charles a DB6 MkII Volante on his 21st birthday – the first of several Aston Martins the heir to the throne would own in coming years. And in late 1969 Tadek Marek's superb all-alloy 5.3-litre V8 was finally installed under the bonnet of the DBS to create the £7,000 DBS V8. Early fuel-injected versions were the supercars of their day – 0–60mph in less than 6 seconds and a top speed of over 160mph (257km/h). As *Autocar* reported in July 1971: "*There can be no doubt that the Aston Martin DBS V8 is one of the fastest cars we have ever tested.*"

For Sir David Brown – knighted in 1968 for services to industry – it should have been cause for quiet satisfaction. But the early 1970s were a period of political and economic uncertainty, and for a perennially financially challenged company like Aston Martin the omens were not good. With increasingly poor finances and floundering sales, Sir David faced the prospect of having to sell his beloved car company.

# TROUBLED TIMES

RKX 700M

# ASTON'S DARKEST HOUR

Aston Martin's finances have often teetered on the brink, but in the mid-1970s the unthinkable happened and the factory doors were closed. A new team brought it back from the brink and initiated a number of new models, including a space-age saloon called the Lagonda.

It was his fellow board members in the parent David Brown Corporation who eventually forced Sir David to sell both the tractor division and Aston Martin Lagonda. The Newport Pagnell concern was sold in February 1972 to Company Developments Ltd, a Birmingham-based consortium of businessmen, for just £100 – for the name, the stock, the buildings and for taking on the £5m debt.

Some feared that an asset-stripping exercise would follow, but the new owners did seem keen to make a fist of car production. Under new chairman William Willson, the DBS and DBS V8 resumed production with revised, single-headlight front-end styling and the DB name dropped from the sales literature. They would now be known as the AM Vantage and AM V8 respectively.

OPPOSITE: William Willson (right) with the long-retired Bert Bertelli.

Naming the lower-powered model 'Vantage' was an odd decision, given that the badge had previously stood for the more powerful variants, but in fact it was just a stop-gap model to use up the remaining stock of straight-six engines. The last of 70 examples left Newport Pagnell in July 1973. Meanwhile the troublesome fuel injection system of the V8 was replaced with carburettors, which required a longer and taller bulge in the bonnet, complete with gaping air intake.

The £9,057 AM V8 was soon the company's only offering, so it had to be good. *Motor* magazine's road testers tried it in 1974 and found it much to their liking. At the time it was the fastest production car produced in Britain, and "*with its outstanding handling and braking perhaps one of the safest*". The 5.3-litre gave 0–60mph in 5.7 seconds, 155mph (249km/h) and overall fuel consumption of 13.2mpg (21.4 l/100km). This was all enough to leave the competition in the form of the Jensen Interceptor, Maserati Indy, Jaguar E-type, BMW 3.0 CSL and Lamborghini Espada trailing in its tyre smoke, though the testers were not so keen on the 'he-man' clutch weight, massive turning circle, or indifferent air-conditioning.

Sales, though, had been badly affected by the oil embargo following the 1972 Arab–Israeli War. Luxury cars that could barely top 13mpg were not in great demand. Then from 1 January 1974 the UK was put on a three-day week to conserve coal supplies. A 50mph (80km/h) speed limit was introduced, queues at the petrol pumps were the norm and the classic Mini became a bestseller again.

The underlying problem for Aston, though, was not even the V8's 13mpg/21.7 l/100km thirst, but the years of failing to keep up with US emissions laws and lacklustre exports; out of 296 cars built in 1973, only 46 went abroad. Choosing to forgo 1974 US certification, Aston went all-out to get its hand-built aluminium 5.3-litre V8 engine fit for 1975 and beyond, but the gruelling 50,000-mile (80,000km) test would cost big money, which the company did not have.

On 30 December 1974, Aston Martin Lagonda declared itself voluntarily insolvent. Production was halted and workers returning from their Christmas and New Year breaks found they were without jobs. As 1975 dawned at Newport Pagnell, the factory was padlocked and half-finished V8s were left on the production line to gather dust.

As the Aston Martin Owners Club organized a "*Save Aston Martin*" campaign and schoolboys donated their pocket money, a bearded man smoking a pipe was 'papped' at Newport Pagnell. The mystery visitor was identified as 35-year-old American businessman Peter Sprague, chairman of the California-based National Semiconductor Corporation and the lifestyle store chain Design Research.

BELOW: Partially built AM V8s gather dust on the production line at Newport Pagnell after the factory was forced to close in December 1974, though servicing continued on the other side of Tickford Street.

BELOW: Press launch of the Lagonda at the Bell Inn, Aston Clinton. No one had ever seen anything like it, and the car was front-page news around the world.

Sprague joined forces with Canadian George Minden, the Rolls-Royce and Aston distributor for Eastern Canada, to mount a rescue, and the pair were later joined by English businessmen Alan Curtis – who would soon become managing director, later chairman – and Denis Flather. Between them they raised £1.7 million and on 23 June 1975, Aston Martin came into its sixth ownership (thus far) with the formation of Aston Martin Lagonda (1975) Ltd.

Plans were immediately put in hand to revitalize the company, and in a move that still seems audacious today, the new management team quickly gave the go-ahead to a radical-looking four-door from the pen of chief stylist William Towns.

Towns's astonishingly low, futuristic Lagonda was shown to the motoring press at the Bell Inn at Aston Clinton in Buckinghamshire on 12 October 1976, and later that month

it made its public debut at the London motor show at Earl's Court. Around 200 orders were taken right there on the stand. Aston Martin was back in the headlines – for all the right reasons.

The main cheerleader for the car was George Minden. Another key player was Brit Mike Loasby, the engineering director at the time. It was Loasby who was chiefly responsible for packaging the V8 engine, three-speed automatic gearbox and all the other underpinnings within Towns's uncompromisingly low and angular shape.

It was not an easy birth – and the main culprits for the delays that ensued were the fantastically ambitious electronics, particularly the dashboard with its digital instruments and touch-sensitive switchgear. Slowly but surely the systems were

ABOVE: Prince Philip, Duke of Edinburgh, tries the Lagonda for size (in the 1950s his personal cars had included a bespoke Lagonda 3-litre Drophead Coupé).

ABOVE: The brochure for the V8 Vantage, launched in 1977. With a top speed of around 170mph (274km/h) and 0–60mph in a little over 5 seconds, it was among the world's fastest cars.

sorted, and by the early 1980s the Lagonda became a strong seller for Aston Martin – particularly in the Middle East and North America. By the time it went out of production in 1990, 638 examples had been sold – a very significant contribution when at times AML was building only three or four cars a week.

Another key new model arrived in 1977. While the Lagonda progressed slowly, a small team of engineers led by Mike Loasby developed a high-performance version of the AM V8, to be marketed as the 'Vantage' – the first time the name had been used for a stand-alone model.

The first step, of course, was wringing more power from the 5.3-litre V8 engine. Four twin-choke Webers with 48mm throats rather than the standard car's 42mm instruments were chosen. There would also be bigger inlet valves, revised camshafts and a rerouted, bigger-bore exhaust. While the standard V8 was producing around 320bhp, the Vantage saw that climb to 375bhp at 6,000rpm, with a seriously beefy 380lb-ft of torque at 4,000rpm.

To cope with the extra muscle, the suspension was stiffened with new Koni dampers, there were bigger, vented brake discs, and the tyres were switched to wider Pirelli CN12s. In a rare event for Aston at the time, the team even wangled a session in MIRA's wind tunnel, where they found that drag could be reduced by 10 per cent by faring the headlights and blanking off not just the grille but also the large air scoop on the bonnet with no detriment to either engine cooling or getting air to the Webers, while a deep front air dam and bootlid spoiler reduced lift.

When the Vantage was launched in February 1977, independent tests put its top speed at just a smidge under 170mph (274km/h) with a 0–60mph time of 5.4 seconds. This was properly rapid for the late-1970s, and while the Aston's immense weight (close to two tons fuelled) and prodigious thirst (think low-teens) were acknowledged, road testers of the day loved it. Here was a British supercar more than capable of taking on the Ferrari Berlinetta Boxer, Lamborghini Countach and Porsche 911 Turbo.

The standard V8 was not neglected, though. A revised model, codenamed 'Oscar India' by aviator chairman Curtis,

BELOW: One of the very first Vantages struts its stuff; as well as a substantial increase in power over the regular V8, it also boasted uprated brakes and suspension.

BELOW: A convertible Volante version of the V8 followed the Vantage in June 1978 and became an immediate sales success, especially in the US.

appeared in October 1978, featuring a neat, flicked-up tail, while a more sumptuous interior with lashings of walnut veneer became a popular option. Meanwhile a new Volante convertible had also been launched. Suddenly Aston Martin Lagonda had a full range of cars!

But the most spectacular was yet to come. In March 1980 Aston Martin unveiled a mid-engined supercar, the 'Bulldog', an ultra-low two-seater styled by William Towns with gull-wing doors. Its 5.3-litre V8 boasted twin Garrett turbochargers, giving an estimated 700bhp – enough, claimed the company, for a top speed of well over 200mph (322km/h). The pet project of chairman Curtis, it was originally intended for a limited production run but would remain a one-off (latterly restored in the UK and in 2023 finally achieving

more than its originally advertised 200mph (322km/h) on a Scottish airstrip).

It was Curtis, too, who initiated the next chapter in the Aston Martin saga. While at a Stirling Moss benefit at Silverstone, he met and started chatting to one Victor Gauntlett – and immediately recognized the perfect figurehead for the storied British marque.

Malcolm Victor Gauntlett was born in 1942 and had already served in the RAF when he joined BP aged just 21 and began to make his mark in the oil trade. His relentlessly genial nature concealed a business mind as quick as it was shrewd. He founded his own oil company, Pace Petroleum, in 1972 and, being a lover of both cars and Britain, did not take much persuading to buy into Aston Martin in 1980, purchasing

ABOVE: The V8 saloon lasted from the early '70s to the late '80s and was the cornerstone of the AM range. Here an early car (left) contrasts with a late EFi.

BELOW: The Bulldog supercar undergoes high-speed testing at the MIRA proving ground; the five centrally mounted headlights were revealed when the motorized nose panel dropped down.

OPPOSITE: Bulldog's press reveal at the Bell Inn, Aston Clinton; huge gullwing doors were hydraulically powered. The car would remain a one-off.

a 12.5 per cent share in the company for £500,000. He was running it the following year and would continue to do so throughout the 1980s as executive chairman, backed initially by Tim Hearley of CH Industrials and latterly by the Livanos Greek shipping family.

Gauntlett's contribution to Aston Martin can scarcely be underestimated. The year after he took control, production was less than a car a week. He saw off a boardroom bid to turn the company into a service, parts and restoration business that would have spelled the end for Aston Martin as we know it. He pushed the Lagonda hard in markets it had been designed for and got Aston Martin out of the financial headlines for the wrong reasons and onto the showbiz pages for the right ones, by putting 007 behind the wheel of an Aston for the first time in 20 years (see Chapter 8).

He also got Aston Martin back into motor racing, co-founding Nimrod Racing Automobiles to run a new Group C car in the World Endurance Championship and at Le Mans (see Chapter 7). And he diversified, building up an

BELOW: The fearsome Vantage Zagato, which rekindled Aston Martin's relationship with the Italian design house.

engineering consultancy arm under the Tickford banner, creating everything from tuned Capris and Metros to the interiors of train carriages.

And, by no means least, he rekindled Aston Martin's relationship with Italian design house Zagato, which gladly collaborated on a rebodied, lightweight version of the Vantage supercar.

Around this time, the Vantage received a welcome power increase with the introduction of the 580X – or X-Pack – engine. This had higher-lift camshafts, larger ports to the cylinder heads and a higher compression ratio. Peak power was now 410bhp, or as much as 437bhp with the optional 50 IDF Webers and a sports exhaust. And this was the spec that went into the fearsome Vantage Zagato. With a top speed of 186mph (299km/h), it was the fastest Aston road car yet. The strictly limited run of 50 coupés and 35 convertibles was sold almost immediately, putting much-needed funds into the Aston coffers.

Of the mainstream models, production of the 'Oscar India' V8 ceased in 1986, to be replaced by a new Weber/Marelli fuel-injected car, distinguished by its almost flat bonnet. These were some of the most useable V8s and Aston sold 405 in the three years before production ceased in 1989.

But even as production ticked up as the world recovered from an economic slowdown, Gauntlett was painfully aware of the age of the existing product and the need for something new. And so work began on what would become the Virage, eventually unveiled in 1988.

Even with a new car, Gauntlett saw there was only one route out of the peripatetic, hand-to-mouth existence that the company had led. He knew one more downturn could spell the end. So when a chance meeting with Walter Hayes, the vice-chairman of Ford of Europe, on the 1987 Mille Miglia led to an expression of interest from the Blue Oval, "*I bit their arm off to the ankles*", as he later put it.

Gauntlett would stay as chairman until 1991, long enough to see the Virage into production, and long enough to be satisfied that his idea for a new DB4 would be realized – in the shape of the DB7. He then left, having formed a new oil company called Proteus that he would later sell to Texaco. He died suddenly in 2003, aged just 60. In his character, charm, Englishness and drive, he was in many ways the living embodiment of the Aston Martin brand.

BELOW: Final fruit of the Gauntlett era was the Virage, which on its launch in 1988 replaced the entire V8 range at a stroke.

FORD TO

# THE RESCUE

771 KRA

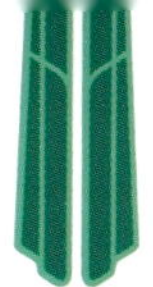

# HENRY SPLASHES THE CASH

Ford might have seemed an unlikely suitor for Aston Martin, but in fact it would prove a benevolent and supportive parent, and in the seductive shape of the DB7 it would produce a model that would sell in numbers hitherto undreamed of.

Walter Hayes was a Ford stalwart and a PR genius (he had been the driving force behind both the GT40 and Cosworth DFV projects) who by the late 1980s had risen all the way through the ranks to become vice-president of Ford Europe. During that chance meeting with Victor Gauntlett on the Mille Miglia, the Aston man had made it abundantly clear that he needed finance to keep AML afloat.

Back in Britain and taking coffee at Henry Ford II's home near Henley, Hayes made a bold proposal: "*Let's buy Aston Martin.*" The timing was right, with the American giant in the market for acquisitions, and with the backing of the Ford family in September 1987, the Big Blue Oval took a 75 per cent share in AML, with the remaining 25 per cent owned equally by the Livanos family and Gauntlett.

OPPOSITE: The Virage took AML into the early 1990s.

A year later the Virage, a car designed to take Aston Martin into the 21st century, was unveiled at the British motor show. The new model was, though, very much a pre-Ford venture. Developed, it was said, for £3.5million – the sort of budget a major carmaker might devote to a new air-con unit alone – it summed up the spirit that kept Aston Martin going through its darkest hours.

Propelled into being largely by the conviction of Gauntlett, the Virage replaced pretty much at a stroke the whole range of classic Aston V8s – saloon, Volante and Vantage variants – with a lineage all the way back to the DBS V8 of 1969. Initial reaction was almost universally positive. The name "Virage" (French for corner, and well-chosen given Aston's long association with Le Mans) flowed naturally from Vantage and Volante. The new shape, by RCA lecturers John Heffernan and Ken Greenley (who beat competition from four other design

BELOW: A Volante version of the Virage followed in 1992; both variants were built in tiny numbers in time-honoured fashion at Newport Pagnell.

ABOVE: The Virage interior followed a familiar recipe, with acres of Connolly hide and lashings of walnut veneer; a modern twist was a single-piece electronic instrument panel.

studios), was not classically beautiful, but it did have presence, and it was convincingly modern – a genuine departure from the old-school Astons, with clean lines and flush glass.

The new skin – still largely hand-formed in aluminium – disguised the fact that underneath was an evolution of the familar steel platform that supported the departing V8s. There was plenty that was new, however. The rear suspension was re-engineered with large cast-aluminium A-frames replacing the old trailing arms to save weight and better isolate occupants from bumps and road noise. Inside were the expected acreages of Wilton carpet, Connolly leather and walnut veneer, but the dials were now on one flat VDU panel with a trip computer in the centre fascia; there were heated seats with electric adjustment and memory, heated front and rear windscreens, and an infrared anti-theft system.

BELOW: The by-now ageing 5.3-litre V8 was given a crucial upgrade for the Virage with four-valve cylinder heads and new engine management to keep pace with emissions regs.

The big news, though, was under the bonnet: still a 5.3-litre V8, but now with four rather than two valves per cylinder, the new heads designed by Callaway Engineering in the US and crucial to improve the V8's efficiency, reduce emissions and make it saleable in all key markets. A new management system was devised for the Weber-Marelli electronic fuel injection and the exhausts were fitted with catalysts for the first time.

Power and torque peaks were 330bhp and 350lb-ft, enough for Aston to claim 0–60mph in the mid-5 seconds and a top speed of 155mph (249km/h). It was a fine achievement for Newport Pagnell, particularly as the company was yet to fully enjoy the financial benefits of Ford's share acquisition, and in the early months a healthy waiting list formed, despite the strong £120,000 price tag.

Ford and Aston Martin even felt sufficiently emboldened to return once more to endurance racing, and in 1989 a new racing team would compete in the World Sportscar

Championship with a 6-litre carbon-chassis Group C car known as the AMR-1 (see Chapter 7).

When Gauntlett resigned in 1991, Hayes took over as chairman. One of his first moves was to set in motion plans for a new, more affordable model. Another was to invite Sir David Brown, long-retired and living in Monte Carlo, to become honorary life president of AML – and persuade him to agree to the use of 'DB' for future models.

Sir David was pleased to be welcomed back into the Aston fold and lived just long enough to see the DB7 – the first Aston to wear his initials in more than 20 years – make its debut at the Geneva show in March 1993. He died that September, aged 89, safe in the knowledge that his legacy was secure.

The DB7 could not come soon enough. After the initial euphoria around the Virage died down, demand had tailed off. The Works Service department at Newport Pagnell had answered the need for something a little stronger with

BELOW: Offered by the Works Service department at Newport Pagnell, the special-order wide-bodied 6.3-litre version of the Virage developed 500bhp.

ABOVE: An early 1990s Vantage prepares to receive its monstrous twin-supercharged 5.3-litre V8. With 550bhp, it was at the time the world's most powerful production engine.

a 465bhp 6.3-litre conversion, and 1992 had also seen the introduction of a three-door Virage Shooting Brake and the debut of the Virage Volante convertible.

Then the following year came a real monster, the 500bhp twin-supercharged Vantage. Transformed visually and dynamically from the slightly underwhelming Virage, it was an old-school behemoth with a measured top speed of 186mph (299km/h) and a 0–100mph time, despite a kerb weight of almost two tons, of just 10.1 seconds. Aston was back in the supercar business. The new Vantage was later further tuned by Works for a 600bhp and 600lb-ft upgrade. Fuel consumption? 15mpg at a gentle cruise, 5mpg if you were pressing on.

But these 'V-cars', for all their brutal magnificence, were still built in tiny numbers. Hayes understood that Ford needed the venerable Aston brand to pay its way and forge a future.

This called for a cheaper model, able to be built in greater numbers, and a rummage through the corporate cupboard of Ford's Premier Automotive Group uncovered just the starting point – an abandoned proposal for a Jaguar XJS replacement.

Designer Ian Callum reworked the ingredients into a svelte and credible Aston Martin shape. Under the bonnet was an AJ16 Jaguar straight-six engine, which gained an Eaton supercharger to help extract 335bhp from the 3.2-litre capacity. Tom Walkinshaw Racing (TWR) carried out the development and ran the factory at Bloxham, Oxfordshire, where the DB7 would be built.

When the DB7 made its debut at the 1993 Geneva salon, it was acclaimed as 'Car of the Show'. It was soon clear that Aston Martin had a substantial hit on its hands. The following year, Ford acquired the rest of the company, confident that the winged badge had a big future. Walter Hayes retired then, his place in Aston history assured.

BELOW: Designer Ian Callum found the very best way to skin a cat when he turned an unloved Jaguar proposal into the much-admired and highly successful DB7.

OVERLEAF: A twin-supercharged Vantage in full flight, its mighty 550lb-ft of torque making light work of the rear tyres.

L953 JKN

In 1995, for the first time ever, Aston Martin Lagonda delivered more than 700 new cars in a single year – and it was almost all down to the DB7. It would be made in bigger numbers than any Aston before it, with 2,451 six-cylinder models leaving the factory before the V12 version replaced them and took production to its 2003 end. In total, 7,091 were built, including the soft-top Volante model, which was launched in 1996 and marked Aston Martin's return to the North American market.

The company was now being run by respected engineer Robert Dover – Bob to his colleagues – who had arrived from Jaguar. The first visible fruit of his tenure was an exciting new concept car, Project Vantage, unveiled at the 1998 Detroit auto show.

This was conceived as a potential new flagship model, and its stunning lines were the work of Ian Callum, inspired by the immortal DB4 GT Zagato of the early 1960s. Underneath the bonnet was a 5.9-litre V12 engine that had originally been designed for a Ford supercar concept but would now find a new home with Aston Martin. Appetites were well and truly whetted.

In fact that V12 engine, now fully productionized and making 420bhp, would appear first in the DB7 Vantage, launched in 1998. Ian Callum had given the '7 a successful restyle, while underneath the skin the chassis and brakes were uprated to cope with the extra performance, the top speed rocketing from 157mph (253km/h) to 185mph (298km/h) and the 0–60mph time falling to 4.9 seconds.

The new model cost £92,500, a mere £7,500 more than the six-cylinder DB7, which saw demand for the in-line six (i6) evaporate pretty much immediately. Suddenly Aston was selling more than 1,000 cars a year. Just as significantly, the Vantage had been an in-house Aston Martin engineering project rather than a TWR one like the original 'i6' DB7. That was key to convincing Ford bosses to invest in Aston Martin – massively, in fact, including in a brand-new factory…

Bob Dover's stint as CEO ended in 2000 when he was appointed chairman of Land Rover, his replacement the former Porsche product design boss Dr Ulrich Bez. Another exciting chapter was about to begin, and one that would see Aston Martin scale further unprecedented heights.

Born in 1943 and raised in the Stuttgart suburb of Bad Cannstatt, Bez had joined Porsche as an apprentice, then studied aeronautical engineering. With a doctorate from the technical University of Berlin, he pursued a varied career that saw him in senior roles at BMW, Porsche, Daewoo and Ford. Vehicle research and development were Dr Bez's forté, and it was these well-honed skills that would see him lead a dynamic era at Aston Martin after he joined as CEO and chairman in 2000.

BELOW: In 1998 Aston Martin launched the Vantage version of the DB7, its all-new Ford-sourced 5.9-litre V12 engine giving it near-supercar levels of performance.

Welcome to
NEWPORT
PAGNELL
Home to
ASTON MARTIN LAGONDA

While work on turning Project Vantage into the new production flagship continued, Bez prepared to relocate Aston Martin to the first purpose-built factory in its history. Two years later he would be showing members of the media around the spectacular new Gaydon headquarters – a strikingly stylish facility in which to build a reinvented range of cars.

Meanwhile, at Newport Pagnell in 2000, the 5,016th and final Aston Martin powered by the classic Tadek Marek-designed V8 left the Tickford Street factory after a production run that had lasted three decades. It had reached its ultimate form in the V600 version of the supercharged Vantage, with monster outputs of 600bhp and 600lb-ft of torque. A final run of 40 'Le Mans' editions, built to celebrate 40 years since Aston Martin won the 24 Hours, saw it go out in fine style.

ABOVE: The Project Vantage concept at the Millbrook proving ground with, from left to right, AML boss Bob Dover, Ford CEO Jac Nasser and designer Ian Callum.

OPPOSITE: Newport Pagnell had been the home of Aston Martin since the mid-50s, but a new factory was now in the pipeline.

# A FRESH

# START

LE03 PKN

# THE GAYDON ERA

A visionary boss, a brand-new purpose-built factory, a completely new range of sports cars that would bring Aston Martin firmly into the 21st century and a revitalized motorsport programme – Aston was entering a new golden age.

The new factory at Gaydon was taking shape quickly, but Newport Pagnell was to produce one final, great Aston Martin. Project Vantage was unveiled at the 2001 Geneva motor show, now fully realized as the V12 Vanquish, AML's new flagship car.

With a radical (partly Lotus-developed) platform that combined extruded, bonded aluminium with composites, a six-speed paddleshift transmission (Aston's first) and a more vocal, 460bhp version of the DB7's V12, all wrapped in superplastic-formed aluminium panels, the Vanquish was an important marker for Aston Martin. The new construction method gave a stiff and relatively lightweight platform for the suspension to work from, the suspension in turn facilitating GT levels of comfort with real composure. The automated manual transmission, despite initial teething problems, was

OPPOSITE: The V12 Vanquish, a new flagship for a new millennium.

ABOVE: The DB7 Zagato was the third collaboration between Aston Martin and styling house Zagato, and featured the latter's signature 'double bubble' roof.

another step into the modern age for Aston, and the 5.9-litre V12 engine was simply glorious. For extra allure, the Vanquish was also the latest Bond car, appearing in *Die Another Day* with Pierce Brosnan as 007 (see Chapter 8).

There was a final rush of activity around the Bloxham-built DB7, too. In 2001 Ulrich Bez and Andrea Zagato met over dinner at the Pebble Beach Concours and hatched a plan for a third-generation Aston Martin Zagato – the DB7 Zagato would be announced in 2002. Later that year and powered by a revised V12 engine, the most sporting version of the DB7 – the 435bhp GT – was launched at the British motor show.

However, from 2003 the epicentre of Aston Martin Lagonda would be the brand-new factory at Gaydon in Warwickshire. And its first model would be something very special – and very significant – indeed.

When the world's press descended on Nice in March 2004 for the driving debut of the DB9, they were attending one of the most important launches in the company's history. Not only was the DB9 the replacement for the DB7 – then the marque's bestselling car yet – it also embodied a whole new manufacturing regime that would underpin the future of the company and its new factory.

We had seen extensive use of aluminium in an Aston's superstructure before, but the original Vanquish was a complex construction of aluminium and carbon fibre and of course still largely hand-built at Newport Pagnell. The DB9 embraced entirely modern manufacturing processes and introduced the

BELOW: The DB9 was a classical, front-engined GT car in the best Aston tradition, combining timeless good looks with thoroughly modern construction and the now-familiar V12 engine.

BELOW: 2005 saw the V8 Vantage name revived, but now for the new entry-level model. The compact two-seater would go on to become the bestselling Aston yet.

so-called VH (Vertical Horizontal) platform – essentially a way of spinning a whole range of cars from the same basic structure and many shared components.

The DB9 was the first of the new breed, its bonded aluminium monocoque and all-wishbone suspension owing absolutely nothing to the DB7. It was not entirely new, though. The magnificent 5.9-litre V12 engine was carried over from the DB7 Vantage, albeit substantially updated with revised crankshaft, cams, inlet and exhaust manifolds and management system. Peak outputs were 450bhp and 420lb-ft of torque (compared with 420bhp and 400lb-ft for the DB7 Vantage).

New(ish) for the DB9 was Touchtronic 2, a six-speed version of the five-speed ZF torque-converter automatic transmission from the DB7 Vantage but now with the

facility to flick between ratios using paddles mounted on the steering column.

The DB9 was extremely well received – polished, completely up to date, a no-excuses sporting GT. The bodywork, shaped initially by Ian Callum and, after the Scot had left to join Jaguar, refined by his successor, Henrik Fisker, took themes first seen on the DB7 and Vanquish and moulded them into something thoroughly contemporary and yet – as the passing years have proved – timelessly beautiful. It would even spawn a highly successful race car, the DBR9 (see Chapter 7).

Aston Martin was suddenly on a roll, and hot on the heels of the DB9 came the V8 Vantage. The new 'affordable' Aston had a starting price of £79,995, bringing the brand within reach of a wider audience and clearly designed to appeal to the same market as Porsche's evergreen 911.

The car was revealed in concept form at the 2003 Detroit show and went into production, visually little-changed, in October 2005 – the second model to be built on the highly adaptable 'VH' platform. Its 4.3-litre quad-cam V8 was based on a Jaguar unit but comprehensively reworked, including a dry-sump lubrication system, variable valve timing on the inlet camshaft, and a bypass valve in the exhaust that clicked open at 4,500rpm to help the V8 find its voice. In standard form it made 380bhp, enough for Aston to claim 4.8 seconds for the 0–60mph sprint and a top speed of 175mph (282km/h). Transmission-wise, all early cars had a traditional Graziano six-speed manual transaxle, but from the 2007 model year (that is, from late 2006) an automated manual, dubbed Sportshift, was available as a cost option.

A Roadster version arrived in 2007, and for the 2009 model year came a capacity increase to 4.7 litres, lifting peak power to 420bhp with a commensurate uplift in torque, accompanied

BELOW: A muscled-up DB9 with a thumping 510bhp, the DBS replaced the Mk1 Vanquish as production flagship in 2007.

by new Bilstein dampers, an improved gearchange linkage and various other tweaks.

Meanwhile, with the V12 Vanquish reaching the end of its production run, Aston Martin launched a new flagship in 2007, the DB9-based DBS, thus resurrecting a name from the late 1960s. With power ramped up to 510bhp, more aggressive styling by new design director Marek Reichman and harder-edged dynamics, the DBS was Mr Hyde to the DB9's Dr Jekyll and gained extra cachet when it debuted as Bond's new company car in *Casino Royale* (*see* Chapter 8).

AML was on an all-time high. In 2007, it sold a record 7,200 cars and earned £92 million. Meanwhile, owner Ford had decided it was time to sell.

The new owners would be a consortium led by David Richards, the chairman of race and rally specialists Prodrive, who had formed a close relationship with AML when his Banbury-based company took on the racing activities of Aston Martin, starting with the DBR9. Richards later told the story:

> *"There was a customer in from America to buy a race car. He [the investment banker John Sinders] was staying the night so I took him out to dinner, over which he raised the subject of Aston Martin being for sale and what my thoughts were. I expressed some concern that the race programme rather depended on who came along next. His response was 'Well why don't you buy it?'*
>
> *"I responded by pointing out there was about a $1 billion difference between my means and the ability to buy it, but he replied: 'I'll get you the money. It won't be a problem.' True to his word, albeit after a few changes of direction and hoops to jump through, he finally did it. That's how I came to lead the consortium that bought the company."*

The consortium included Sinders himself and two Kuwaiti companies – Investment Dar and Adeem Investment – and on 12 March 2007 they purchased Aston Martin for £475 million, though Ford kept a stake, valued at £40 million. With the sale, Richards became AML chairman, with Ulrich Bez remaining as CEO.

A new era was beginning at Gaydon, while across the Midlands at Newport Pagnell the old factory buildings on one side of Tickford Street were demolished, leaving Aston Martin Works – the sales, service and restoration operation – as AML's sole presence in the town. In total, 12,879 Aston Martins had been built there between 1955 and 2007, and Newport Pagnell would continue to be known as the spiritual home of the marque.

BELOW: Aston Martin Lagonda moved into its new, purpose-built factory and HQ at Gaydon, Warwickshire, in September 2003.

At Gaydon, the opening ceremony for a new design studio included the first sighting of the V12 Vantage RS Concept – a mouthwatering preview of what would become the V12 Vantage. But soon the chill winds of a worldwide economic recession began to bite, and in December 2008 the company announced it was cutting its workforce from 1,850 to 1,250 as sales faltered.

Undaunted, Dr Bez pressed ahead with ambitious plans to expand the model range. In 2009 Aston Martin launched the Rapide saloon, a four-door (five including the rear hatch) four-seater powered by a 470bhp version of the V12 engine and designed to steal sales from Porsche's successful Panamera model. Dr Bez envisaged annual sales of 2,000 cars – too many for Gaydon to cope with, so production was originally outsourced to Magna Steyr in Austria. In fact the Rapide never sold more than a few hundred a year and in 2012 production relocated to the UK.

BELOW: 2009 saw the launch of the first four-door Aston Martin (five if you count the rear hatch) in the handsome shape of the V12-engined Rapide.

ABOVE: The fastest, most exotic and most expensive roadgoing Aston Martin yet seen, the One-77 featured a 750bhp version of AML's 5.9-litre V12 and all-carbon construction.

AML also revealed the no-expense-spared One-77 hypercar, the world's most powerful naturally aspirated (that is, non-supercharged) road car, with a stupendous 750bhp version of the V12 engine, a top speed of 220mph (354km/h) and an equally gobsmacking £1.15 million price tag. Strictly limited to 77 examples, it was a compelling take on the ultimate Aston.

Scarcely less exciting – and slightly more affordable – was the V12 Vantage, now unleashed in production form with the 510bhp V12 from the DBS crammed into the compact Vantage bodyshell, in the process creating one of the most exciting Aston Martin road cars of all time. There was even a proposed revival of the Lagonda brand, although the huge and ungainly SUV concept that bore the venerated badge got a decidedly lukewarm reaction.

ABOVE: The V12 Vantage, here pursued by its Zagato-bodied sibling, packed Aston's largest engine into its most compact bodyshell, with predictably thrilling results.

There was more head-scratching at the 2010 Geneva motor show, when Aston unveiled its 1.3-litre Cygnet luxury compact. Not since the 1976 Lagonda wedge had a car produced by Aston Martin elicited such an extreme reaction. People either loved or hated the baby Aston.

Ulrich Bez's original plan was that the Cygnet would be sold only to existing Aston owners, but when they decided it was not for them the order book was thrown open to all. Still potential buyers baulked. The biggest hurdle was the price –

£30,995 (without options) was pretty much three times the price of the base version of the Toyota iQ city car on which the Cygnet was based. Dr Bez's dream was to sell up to 4,000 a year. In fact, the Cygnet sold so slowly that Aston pulled the plug after less than three years, by which time just 789 had been built. Ironically, those cars are now increasingly sought-after by city-driving Aston fans.

AML was on much firmer ground with a new Zagato collaboration, this time based on the V12 Vantage. The V12 Zagato made its debut at the 2011 Villa d'Este Concorso d'Eleganza and was a hit with press and public alike. The same was true of the second-generation Vanquish, which combined strikingly sculpted carbon-fibre bodywork with a 565bhp V12 and replaced the DBS as the production flagship in 2012.

A thoroughly updated DB9, now with 510bhp, revised bodywork and carbon-ceramic brake discs as standard, was launched for the 2013 model year, and when the uprated

BELOW: Dr Bez's baby, the Cygnet, added Aston styling cues and Aston standards of interior luxury to the Toyota iQ city car.

OVERLEAF: The Zagato family gained its latest member in 2011 with the rebodied V12 Vantage. While familiar Zagato design signatures were present, the car was in fact designed by Aston's in-house team.

V12 ZAGATO

ABOVE: The 2013 centenary timeline at Kensington Palace featured every model from A3, the oldest surviving Aston, to the then-new CC100 Speedster concept.

Rapide S replaced the original Rapide with its own facelift and power up from 470 to 550bhp, it completed a thoroughly refreshed model line-up.

It was a strong position from which to celebrate Aston Martin's centenary in 2013 – 100 years since Bamford and Martin had formed their tiny company in Henneker Mews. And AML did it in fine style, with a 'timeline' of 100 iconic models to dazzle the crowds in the grounds of Kensington Palace, the unveiling of the retro-styled CC100 Speedster concept, and the launch of the V12 Vantage S – the fastest series-production Aston Martin yet, with 565bhp and a claimed top speed of 205mph (330km/h).

There was also a significant new development that had the potential to shape the marque's second century: Aston Martin signed a letter of intent to form a technical partnership with

Mercedes-AMG GmbH. According to press reports the deal would see:

> *"... the joint development of a new V8 engine, but also give Aston a chance to use some of Daimler's next-generation electronic architecture. In return, Mercedes' parent company Daimler will take a five per cent stake in Aston Martin."*

It was also the end of the Ulrich Bez era, the visionary German standing down as CEO at the end of 2013, though he would continue for some time as non-executive chairman. How would the Bez era be remembered? For taking Aston from Newport Pagnell to an all-new facility at Gaydon. Making the transition from Ford ownership to that of a Kuwaiti-led consortium. Completing the transformation from quaint British carmaker to profitable brand powerhouse. But fittingly and most importantly, for some truly great cars.

BELOW: Zagato showed it was still very much in the business of rebodying Astons with two centenary-themed one-offs, a DB9-based Spyder (foreground) and DBS-based Coupé.

# FAST FORWARD

# SECOND CENTURY PLAN

With its centenary celebrations still fresh in the memory, Aston Martin entered its second century with a new CEO and ambitious plans to broaden the marque's appeal with its first SUV, all leading up to a flotation on the London Stock Exchange.

In September 2014, 12 months after Ulrich Bez stood down, Aston Martin announced it had a new boss – 51-year-old British-born Dr Andrew 'Andy' Palmer. Behind the scenes, Dr Bez took on a new, ambassadorial role, while David Richards remained in charge of Aston Martin Racing but relinquished his involvement with the road car operation. And so Aston Martin began its second century.

Palmer joined from Nissan, where he had juggled a dizzying number of roles, including chief planning officer and executive vice-president. Previously he had worked his way up through the Rover Group to become transmissions chief engineer. Senior motoring industry insiders and commentators reckoned him one of the sharpest minds in the business.

On the product front, 2014 finally saw the return of

OPPOSITE: The Rapide-based Taraf was the first Lagonda since the '70s wedge.

Lagonda in the shape of the Rapide-based Taraf saloon, Marek Reichman's design paying loose homage to the 1976 William Towns wedge, while Vanquish and Rapide benefited from new eight-speed gearboxes and a number of other refinements.

For sheer shock and awe, though, little could top the track-only Vulcan hypercar. This spectacular 7-litre 800+bhp V12-engined, all-carbon, £1.5m (plus local taxes) monster was billed as "*what happens when Aston Martin is unleashed from the constraints of making road-legal cars*". Just 24 examples would be built – at least one of which was later converted for road use!

The Vulcan was the work of AML's Special Projects Department, then a relatively new addition to the company's

engineering capability. David King's small team had become hugely skilled and experienced in delivering low-volume, high-profile projects including the Lagonda Taraf and the DB10 Bond cars (see Chapter 8), but the Vulcan was their most ambitious challenge yet.

It was unveiled at the 2015 Geneva show, along with the GT12 (a track-biased hardcore version of the V12 Vantage) and a bold new electric 'crossover' concept called DBX, which hinted at both a future SUV and the inevitability of electric propulsion for future Astons. The DBX concept was the first really significant fruit of Andy Palmer's leadership. "*Like everybody else, we can't stand still,*" he told reporters.

BELOW: The Vulcan was AML's track-only hypercar, built in tiny numbers, eye-wateringly expensive and designed as a trackday toy for the mega-wealthy.

ABOVE: The first of a new generation of Aston Martin road cars, moving the game on from the VH era, was the DB11, launched with a new, 5.2-litre twin-turbo V12.

The first major new production car of the Palmer era, however, was the DB11, replacement for the DB9 and launched in 2016. With a new twin-turbo V12 and cutting-edge aerodynamics and electronics, the DB11 was the first of a new generation of Astons and the first product of AML's 'Second Century' plan. It was also the fastest, most powerful and most fuel-efficient 'DB' road car yet, with prices starting at £154,000.

The DB11's new 592bhp 5.2-litre twin-turbo V12 engine had the novelty of cylinder deactivation, which meant you effectively got two engines in one: a 2.6-litre single-turbo 296bhp straight-six during small throttle openings (such as a steady-state cruise), with the full dozen cylinders coming seamlessly on stream when more power and torque were required.

The platform was still all-aluminium but had many more – and more complicated – aluminium pressings than the previous VH generation. Aerodynamic novelties included a new wing vent, or 'curlicue', designed to release high-pressure air from the front wheelarch to reduce front-end lift. At the rear a jet of air was released from the trailing edge of the rear deck. This 'AeroBlade' mimicked the effect of a rear spoiler, but without the drag or the aesthetic challenges. Just as importantly, and thanks to the technical partnership with Daimler, the DB11's cockpit featured much-improved infotainment systems.

Aston watchers were also intrigued by the announcement of a new hypercar project, a joint venture between Aston Martin and Red Bull Racing Advanced Technologies. The new car, conceived by F1 designer Adrian Newey, was codenamed AM-RB 001, and early full-size models suggested something more akin to a race car than a road car, with extreme aerodynamics and talk of F1 levels of performance.

The other big news in 2016 was the announcement that a brand-new factory would be built at a former Ministry of Defence site at St Athan in South Wales, where three giant 'super hangars' would be converted into a production facility for the forthcoming DBX, Aston's first SUV. St Athan would take the lion's share of a massive £200 million investment

BELOW: Meanwhile, Aston Martin Works at Newport Pagnell saw a return to car production with a series of limited-edition 'Continuation' models, starting with a run of DB4 GTs.

programme aimed at more than doubling production in five years – the plan was for the new factory to produce 5,000 cars a year, lifting total annual sales to around 12,000.

It was certainly an ambitious plan. By the mid-2010s total AML production had dropped to around 3,500 cars a year, a far cry from the 7,200 cars sold in 2007, and Palmer identified the need to attract more female buyers to the brand – something he hoped the DBX would help achieve.

In another outpost of the AML empire, it was announced in 2017 that car production was returning to Newport Pagnell with a run of DB4 GT 'Continuation' cars – 25 brand-new examples of the late-50s classic to add to the 75 originally built, completing the 100 cars originally planned. Further continuation runs of DB4 GT Zagatos and – most thrillingly for grown-up schoolboys everywhere – Bond-spec DB5s complete with working gadgets would follow. With price tags in

BELOW: Second in the series of Continuation models was the DB4 GT Zagato. Just 19 were built and customers could buy them only as part of a pair with the all-new DBS-based GT Zagato (opposite).

ABOVE: The other half of the DBZ Centenary Collection, conceived to celebrate Zagato's 100th birthday in 2019, was the all-new DBS GT Zagato. Price for the pair? A cool £6m (plus local taxes).

the millions (the DB5 was priced at £3.3m in the UK), and each edition quickly sold out, these reborn icons would provide a very welcome boost to the AML coffers over the next few years.

Staying in this rarefied atmosphere, more details emerged about the Newey-designed hypercar, including the fact that it would have a 1,000bhp Cosworth-designed 6.5-litre naturally aspirated V12 and would be called Valkyrie. And in the summer of 2017 AML unveiled its latest Zagato collaboration, an unprecedented 'family' of four cars – Coupé, Volante, Speedster and Shooting Brake – all based on the Mk2 Vanquish.

Back in the mainstream, autumn 2017 saw the launch of an all-new V8 Vantage, with styling derived from the DB10 Bond car (see Chapter 8) and an AMG-sourced twin-turbocharged 503bhp 4-litre V8, giving a 195mph (314km/h)

ABOVE: The first Aston to bear the full fruit of AML's tie-up with Mercedes was the new V8 Vantage launched for the 2018 model year with an AMG-sourced twin-turbo V8.

OPPOSITE: The fastest and most powerful series-production Aston yet was the 2018 DBS Superleggera, based on the DB11 but with a 715bhp version of the twin-turbo V12.

top speed. This new 'entry-level' Aston came with a £120,000 price tag. It had a tough act to follow. The car it replaced, the VH-generation Vantage, had been in production since the end of 2005 and was the most successful model range in Aston Martin's entire history, with more than 24,000 sold across both V8 and V12 versions.

AML, though, was on a new high. The company announced record profits, driven by sales of the DB11 (now with a new V8 version to go with the V12) and the sold-out quartet of Zagato models. There would soon be a new production flagship, too, the DBS Superleggera, with a muscled-up version of the DB11's body and a 715bhp version of its twin-turbo V12. Sales were approaching 6,500 a year – and there was still DBX to come.

Andy Palmer's ambition seemingly knew no bounds, with plans announced for two further new mid-engined sports cars, tentatively named Valhalla and Vanquish, and not one but two

DBS I

BELOW: The Mk2 Vanquish ran from 2012 to 2018; the run-out 'Ultimate' edition was the last Aston to be powered by the long-lived 5.9-litre naturally aspirated V12.

new Lagondas, an SUV and a saloon, to be built alongside the DBX at St Athan.

It was all leading up to AML's flotation in 2018 on the London Stock Exchange – the first car company to register on the FTSE for 28 years. Alas, the champagne very quickly went flat. With an extremely punchy £5 billion valuation, the initial share price was £19, but within a year they were trading for little over £5.

Brexit did not help; nor did an unexpected slowdown in the key Chinese market, and in June 2019 the company admitted it had overestimated annual sales by as many as 1,000 cars. In October it was forced to raise $150m to keep its ambitious plans on track, at a perilously high interest rate of 12 per cent.

Much now depended on the DBX, which launched in late 2019. With a 542bhp 4-litre twin-turbo V8, four-wheel drive and prices starting at £158,000, it offered sumptuous

accommodation for four adults. And in terms of driving dynamics, road testers put it right at the top of its class. It was a landmark moment for Aston Martin.

And then came Covid-19. On 25 March 2020 production at both Gaydon and St Athan was halted and 75 per cent of staff were furloughed. Dealerships closed and car press launches were postponed. A staggered reopening began in May and it took until midsummer before DBX production was finally in full swing.

In the meantime, partly as a result of the knock-on effects of the pandemic, the share price had dipped as low as just 94 pence – plenty of food for thought for a new executive chairman. Enter the Canadian billionaire and investor Lawrence Stroll. Stroll was no stranger to the automotive world. As well as having his own F1 team, he was a Ferrari

ABOVE: Aston Martin couldn't afford to ignore the worldwide trend towards SUVs and in late 2019 launched the four-wheel-drive DBX with a 542bhp twin-turbo V8.

BELOW: The mid-engined Valhalla is aimed directly at Ferrari customers, its hybrid power train developing a combined 937bhp.

collector and owned the Ferrari concession for Montreal and Eastern Canada. And in January 2020 he led a consortium that would invest £182 million in return for a 16.7 per cent stake in Aston Martin Lagonda. A further £318 million cash infusion through a new rights issue generated a total of £500 million to keep AML afloat.

Stroll immediately committed the company to reducing stock held by dealerships and ultimately returning the marque to a built-to-order strategy more in keeping with a luxury brand. Another key pillar of his vision was the rebranding of his Racing Point Formula 1 team as Aston Martin F1 for the start of the 2021 season.

In May 2020, it was announced that Andy Palmer had stepped down as CEO. In his place, Stroll brought in 54-year-old ex-AMG CEO Tobias Moers. Like Palmer, Moers was a trained engineer who had worked his way through the ranks, and he arrived with a reputation as a forceful leader. At AMG he had led development of the 4-litre twin-turbo V8 that now powered a number of Astons. And that relationship was about to get stronger still. In October 2020, AMG parent Daimler took a 20 per cent stake in AML in return for greater access to engines and technology.

Torchbearer for Moers's 'Project Horizon' road map for the brand was a revamped Valhalla supercar, revealed in summer 2021. First announced as a concept in 2019, the mid-engined 'Son of Valkyrie' was planned to be a continuation of the close technical partnership between Aston and Red Bull, with an all-new turbocharged 3-litre V6 supplemented by hybrid electric.

Valhalla V2 had a number of key revisions. Gone was the in-house-developed V6, replaced by an AMG-sourced twin-turbocharged V8. A new intake system and other detail changes would lift peak power from 720 to 740bhp, while a new 150kW/400V hybrid system employed a pair of electric motors, one on the rear axle just behind the mid-mounted V8 and another at the front, combining to produce 201bhp and endowing the Valhalla with a total of 937bhp. Significantly, it would use an all-new eight-speed DCT twin-clutch transmission (a first for Aston). With full carbon fibre construction, target dry weight was 1,550kg (3,417lb), Aston projecting a 0–60mph time of 2.5sec and a top speed of 217mph (349km/h).

Now all AML had to do was get it into production – and hope it would not take as long as Valkyrie. First seen as a mock-up in 2016, the first customer Valkyries were only now finally

BELOW: After a prolonged gestation, the Valkyrie hypercar began reaching customers in 2021. This is the Spider version, which uses the same 1,000bhp 6.5-litre Cosworth-developed V12 as the closed car.

BELOW: DB12, launched in 2023, was described by AML as a 'super tourer' and with a 671bhp twin-turbo V8 giving 200mph-plus performance, few argued.

being delivered at the end of 2021. In the meantime Aston had announced a Spider version, along with a track-only AMR Pro model, both to be built in tiny numbers, both oversubscribed.

Moers was clearly making waves – his harder-edged F1 Edition of the V8 Vantage, underlining the links to the F1 team, was described as the car the Vantage should have been from the outset. But he was also ruffling feathers: 2021 saw the departure of a number of key personnel, including director of design Miles Nurnberger, chief engineer Matt Becker and head of special operations David King.

The emerging product was still strong, though. March 2022 saw the launch of a V12 version of the Vantage, its 5.2-litre twin-turbo V12 engine producing a cool 700PS (690bhp), good for a top speed of 200mph (322km/h), with 0–60 in 3.4 seconds. It would be the last of that particular sub-genre, said AML, with production limited to just 333 units.

More significantly, given the way the market was going, May 2022 saw the introduction of the DBX707, the world's most powerful luxury SUV with an astonishing 707PS (697bhp) and handling so good that appeared to defy the laws of physics.

But May 2022 also saw the departure of Tobias Moers, who stepped down from the role as a result of "strategic differences" with Lawrence Stroll. In his place as CEO came former Ferrari boss Amedeo Felisa, while ex-Ferrari engineer Roberto Fedeli joined as chief technical officer. Felisa, 76, had been Ferrari CEO from 2008 to 2016 and had previously run product development at Alfa Romeo. "*Nobody knows how to make ultra-luxury performance cars better than Amedeo,*" said Lawrence Stroll. "*He saw the movie, he wrote the script.*"

On the financial front, Saudi Arabia's Public Investment Fund (PIF) took a major stake in AML, and later in 2022 Chinese carmaker Geely joined them (Geely would subsequently increase its stake to 17 per cent, becoming the third largest shareholder after Stroll's Yew Tree consortium and the Saudi PIF).

In 2023, Aston Martin celebrated 110 years with the first of what it called a new generation of sports cars. Billed as a 'super-tourer', combining supercar performance with grand touring capabilities, the DB12, though clearly evolved from the DB11, was particularly notable for its much-improved cabin, which combined a true luxury feel with state-of-the-art interfaces, while a 671bhp version of the AMG-derived

OPPOSITE: The V8 Vantage got a major upgrade for 2024, with revamped looks, a new interior and a hike in power from the 4-litre twin-turbo V8, from 503bhp to an eye-widening 656bhp.

OVERLEAF: Some 100 years and 1,000bhp separate Valkyrie Spider and Razor Blade, though they share the same absolute focus on performance.

twin-turbo V8 took care of the 'super' part of the equation with 0–60mph in 3.6 seconds and a top speed of 202mph (325km/h). In the DB5's sixtieth anniversary year, the latest DB model was an instant hit with buyers and reviewers alike.

By late 2023, the order book for the DB12, continuing high demand for the DBX and the promise of a wholly revised Vantage model for 2024 appeared to have put AML on course to return to pre-2008 levels of production of 7,000-plus vehicles a year, while the heavy pre-tax losses of previous years had been significantly reduced. It was by no means out of the woods, but the signs were encouraging.

Indeed, when the revamped Vantage was revealed in February 2024, it exceeded all expectations, with the wick turned right up on the twin-turbocharged V8 to produce a walloping 656bhp and 590lb-ft of torque – massive increases on the outgoing model's 503bhp and 505lb-ft, promising near-supercar levels of performance. With an aggressive new look and a transformed interior, it gave Aston Martin its strongest offering in years.

And for the future? In June 2023 Aston Martin signed a supply agreement with electric vehicle technologies company Lucid Group. The agreement would see Lucid supply AML with industry-leading electric power trains and battery systems to underpin the company's entire future electrified model range, from hypercars to sports cars, GTs and SUVs. The first plug-in hybrid – the mid-engined Valhalla – was scheduled for 2024, with the first all-electric Aston targeted for launch in 2025.

Back from the brink so many times, but with a legacy that few could match, Aston Martin looked set to continue its journey into a new automotive landscape.

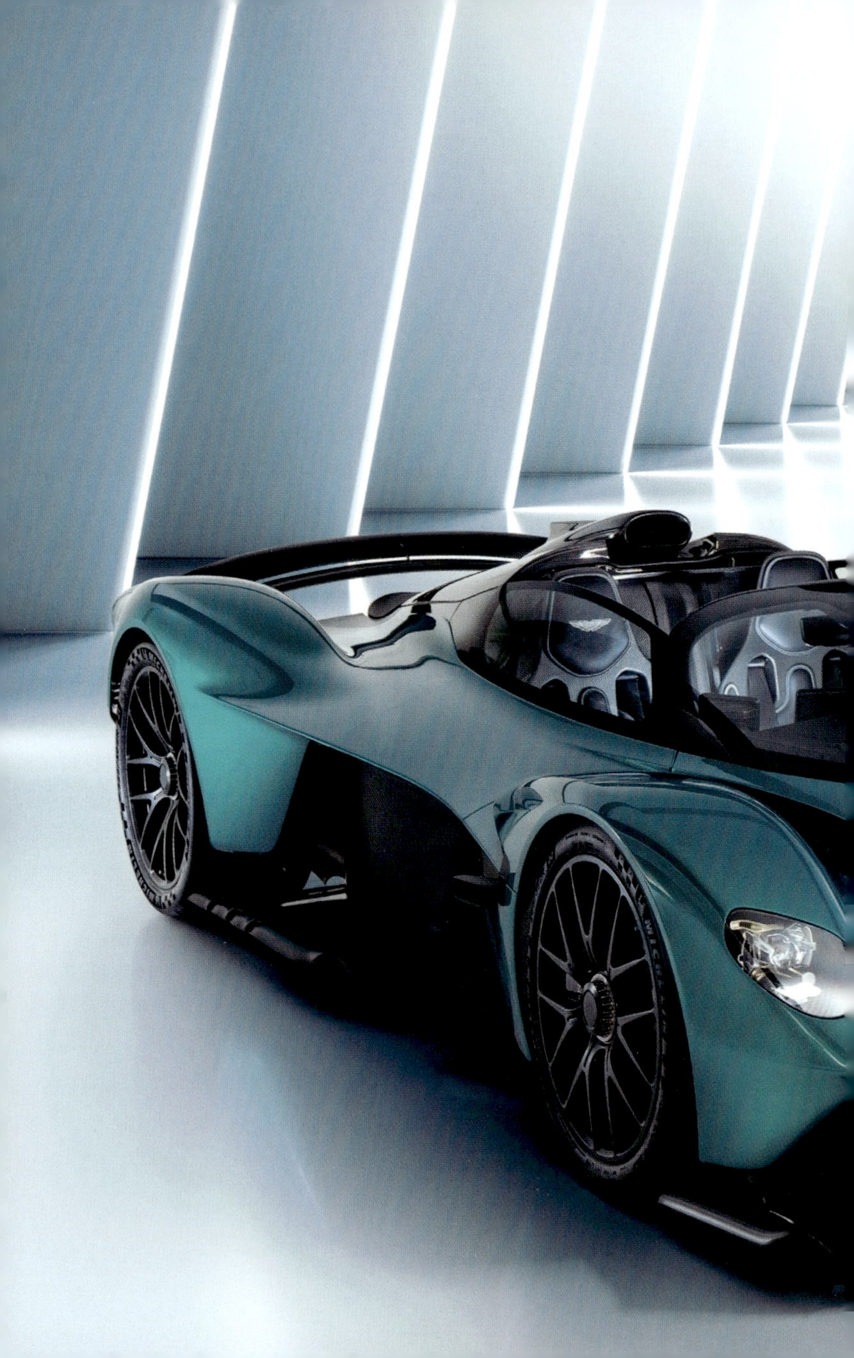

503

# LE MANS AND

# FORMULA 1

509

# THE SPORTING LIFE

Right from the start, Aston Martin was inextricably linked with motorsport – and that close association continues today in both sportscars and Formula 1. Some of its finest hours have been carved out in the heat of endurance racing, and at one circuit in particular.

From the outset in 1913, the *raison d'etre* of Aston Martin was to build fast, high-quality sports cars that could compete in motorsport in the hands of professionals and amateurs alike. Bamford and Martin gave birth to this concept, but it was William Renwick and 'Bert' Bertelli who took it to another level in the late 1920s and early 1930s.

In this period, 24 factory-backed cars – known as the 'team' cars – competed strongly in national races at Brooklands and Donington, and in international events such as the Ulster TT, Mille Miglia, Targa Abruzzo and, of course, Le Mans.

Early successes in the French classic included a class win and fifth place overall in 1931, and further class wins in 1932 and 1933. These did much to cement the reputation of Aston

OPPOSITE: The pretty DB3S was a regular race-winner in the '50s.

BELOW: The DBR1 was built with the express intent of winning Le Mans; exotic construction included a space-frame chassis and a plethora of lightweight alloys.

Martin for building handsome, rugged and rapid cars, pretty much all suited to competition work.

When the team cars LM11, 12 and 14 failed to finish Le Mans in 1934, Bertelli's wife Vera suggested that perhaps their British Racing Green paintwork was not such a lucky colour, so for the TT the entries were painted Italian racing red in the hope of a change of fortunes. It worked. All three finished, winning the team prize, LM15 placing sixth overall. A month later the customer version was shown at Earl's Court, and to reflect its recent success in Northern Ireland it was given a new name – Ulster.

The Ulster would become the definitive Aston of the years before the Second World War, and its greatness was confirmed in 1935 when LM20 finished first in class and third overall at Le Mans. The bond between Aston Martin and the world's most famous endurance race was well and truly established.

Aston Martin's post-war saviour David Brown made no bones about his desire to win Le Mans. It was a dream he pursued from the moment he bought the company in 1947, and the early results were certainly promising. In 1949 a 2 Litre Sports (aka DB1) came eleventh and an early four-cylinder DB2 finished seventh, but more power was on the way with the Lagonda-sourced straight-six engine.

For 1950 the tactical genius John Wyer was put in charge of racing activities and Aston Martin entered three six-cylinder DB2s for Le Mans: two finished first and second in the 3-litre class and fifth and sixth overall. The following year they went even better, finishing third, fifth and seventh to take the first three places in the 3-litre class.

It was not until 1955 that Aston scored its next notable result, a DB3S finishing second overall and once again winning the 3-litre class. While the DB3S was a fine car (the model would score further second places in 1956 and 1958) its road-car origins meant it was heavy compared with the Ferraris and Maseratis of the day. So when Le Mans announced an engine ceiling of 2.5 litres for 1956, that was the cue Aston needed to develop a completely bespoke racer from scratch.

The Ted Cutting-designed DBR1 featured a new 'perimeter' spaceframe, which helped keep weight down to a smidge over 800kg (1,764lb), and at the rear was a new de Dion rear suspension set-up and five-speed, magnesium-cased transaxle. The 'RB6' straight-six engine was a new, all-alloy design with a 60-degree twin-plug cylinder head derived from the final evolution of the DB3S unit. It was lighter and stronger than

BELOW: All finally came good for Aston Martin and the DBR1 in 1959 when the driver pairing of Carroll Shelby and Roy Salvadori scored outright victory at Le Mans.

OPPOSITE: A classical combination: Stirling Moss, Aston DBR1 and Goodwood race circuit on a summer's day.

what had gone before, while a dry sump allowed it to be placed lower in the chassis. Crucially, with a lightweight engine and rear transaxle, weight distribution was nigh-on perfect.

The DBR1 prototype ran strongly on its debut in 1956 before retiring after 21 hours (a DB3S upheld Aston honour, finishing second overall and first in class). But though its pace was obvious, mechanical problems caused retirements in both 1957 and '58.

In 1959, however, the stars finally aligned. Aston threw everything it had at that race, including three DBR1s. Moss set the early pace, but it was DBR1/2, driven by Carroll Shelby and Roy Salvadori that took the flag. There was then the small matter of the World Sportscar Championship, which Moss clinched at Goodwood. For David Brown, champagne never tasted better.

Mission accomplished, Brown disbanded the racing department soon after, but in 1962, under pressure from the

7
TEX

BELOW: Streamlined 'Project cars' flew the flag at Le Mans in the early '60s. This is DP212, the first of the line. Alas, they were to prove fast but mechanically fragile.

dealers for more competition success, Aston Martin returned to Le Mans with the first of the so-called 'Project cars', DP212, a modified DB4GT with a 330bhp 3996cc engine and de Dion rear suspension. Despite taking an early lead, it failed after five hours with piston trouble.

For 1963 two all-new Project cars were built: DP214 would be the first car to exceed 300km/h (186mph) at Le Mans, while DP215 was even quicker, establishing a new record for the fastest-ever front-engined car of 198.5mph (319.4km/h) on the famous Mulsanne Straight. Sadly, for all their speed, neither car finished the race.

In the mid-1960s, Aston Martin's new V8 engine, then still in the development phase, was fitted to a Lola T70 chassis, but the beautiful Lola–Aston was another Did Not Finish. And

in the 1970s Aston dealer Robin Hamilton made a plucky bid for Le Mans glory with a much-modified DBS V8 saloon, RHAM/1 (aka 'The Muncher' because of its appetite for brake discs!). It finished seventeenth overall and third in class in the 1977 race – a commendable result for the tiny outfit.

After his adventures with The Muncher, Robin Hamilton took the momentous decision in 1981 to form an all-new team and commission a purpose-built racing car to challenge for outright victory at Le Mans. Start-up investment came from Hamilton (reportedly to the tune of £125,000) and this was matched by AML chairman Victor Gauntlett. The design of the car was entrusted to Eric Broadley, of Lola T70 and Ford GT40 fame. And so the Aston Martin Nimrod programme was born.

ABOVE: A mid-60s Le Mans entry was this Lola T70 with a prototype version of Aston Martin's V8 engine, then in its early development stages. Sadly the Lola-Aston failed to finish.

ABOVE: The Nimrod was Aston Martin's early '80s entry in the hotly contested Group C category of sportscar racing, here running in third place at the 1982 Le Mans.

As well as the 'factory' team, wealthy Aston enthusiast Viscount Downe bought a customer car and appointed renowned specialist Richard Williams to run this privateer team, drafting in the experienced Ray Mallock to both drive and help develop the car. With a strong driver line-up of Mallock, Simon Phillips and Mike Salmon, the Downe car ran as high as third at Le Mans in 1982 before burnt-out valves slowly dropped them down the order to finish a highly creditable seventh overall. It was to be Nimrod's best result at Le Mans.

Victor Gauntlett and AML financial backer Peter Livanos still had Le Mans ambitions, however, and in late 1987 they were ready to go again. A new company, Proteus Technology Limited, was set up and by 1989 they had everything in place for a proper bid for Le Mans glory with an exciting new Group C car, the carbon fibre-tubbed AMR1.

Alas, its rear-mounted radiators gave too much aerodynamic drag in what was the last 24 Hours to use the full Mulsanne Straight, uninterrupted by chicanes, so where the turbocharged Sauber Mercedes C9s were hitting an incredible 248mph (399km/h), AMR1 could manage only around 217mph (349km/h). Still, while AMR1/03 retired with engine failure, AMR1/01 was eleventh in what was only the car's second race.

Le Mans in 1990 was looking very promising indeed, but then the rules suddenly changed. Now the teams had to use a 3.5-litre F1-type engine. Ford had recently bought both Aston Martin and Jaguar and decided it would be Jaguar's Group C programme that would get Cosworth's 3.5-litre V8. Proteus Technology was wound up and Aston's Group C adventure was over.

It would be 15 years before Aston Martin was ready to go racing seriously again. This time its target was the GT1 class and its weapon was a brand-new racing machine loosely based on the DB9 and developed by Prodrive, whose boss

BELOW: A challenger of the late '80s was the fabulous, carbon-bodied AMR1; its promise would remain unfulfilled when Ford decided to back Jaguar rather than Aston in Group C.

BELOW: Aston returned to winning ways at Le Mans with a new team, the Prodrive-backed Aston Martin Racing, and a brilliant new GT class contender, the DBR9.

David Richards had persuaded the money men to let him run a newly formed Aston Martin Racing division. The brilliant DBR9 scored a win on its debut in the 2005 Sebring 12 Hours, and after two frustrating years at Le Mans took back-to-back class wins in 2007 and 2008. Aston supporters had a new sporting icon.

Suitably encouraged, Aston Martin Racing was ready to go for the top prize. In 2009, 50 years years after it won the 24 Hours outright, Aston Martin would compete for outright honours again, this time with a V12-engined LMP1 car developed with Lola and named DBR1-2, in honour of the 1959 winner. It was a fine race car but it was up against diesel prototypes from the likes of Audi, which the rules at the time favoured. Still, one of the DBR1-2s finished in a commendable fourth place, the first of the petrol-engined cars home.

And if another outright win would remain elusive, the various GT classes became a happy hunting ground for Aston

Martin Racing over the next decade or so. Racing versions of the V8 and V12 Vantage became a dominant force in the World Endurance Championship (WEC), Blancpain GT3 series and a host of national GT series in the UK, Europe, the US and Far East.

And at Le Mans too, of course. In 2017 Aston Martin Racing chalked up a hat-trick of wins in GTE Pro, the top GT class, when the Vantage GTE no.97 beat the Corvettes in a famous final-lap triumph, one of the closest finishes for years.

The end of the decade saw the new AMG-engined generation of Vantage take to the track. In 2020 it stepped out of the shadow of its illustrious forbear and made motorsport history, with Aston Martin Racing and customer team TF Sport expertly steering their cars to twin Le Mans class wins – the factory team scoring a dominant first and third

ABOVE: In 2009 Aston Martin Racing went for outright victory at Le Mans with a mid-engined prototype, the DBR1-2, but fell foul of rules favouring the diesel opposition.

BELOW: Le Mans 2020 and the celebrations begin as AMR Vantages finish first and third in the GTE Pro class, while customer team TF Sport score first place in GTE Am.

in the GTE Pro category, TF Sport achieving an equally impressive victory in GTE Am. With AMR also securing the WEC manufacturers' title and AMR's Nicki Thiim and Marco Sorensen securing the GTE Pro Drivers' world title, it sealed Aston Martin's most successful season in international motorsport since 1959.

The long-running WEC GTE programme ended in 2020, but Aston Martin would continue to support customer teams in various endurance series – and with no little success, including a GTE-Am class win for TF Sport at Le Mans in 2022.

Then in October 2023 came the news all Aston motorsport fans had been waiting for: from 2025 a racing prototype version of the Valkyrie hypercar would be competing for outright victory in top-level endurance racing – including Le Mans. The next pages of history waited to be written.

## FORMULA 1

Compared with its record in endurance racing, Aston Martin had very little form in Formula 1 until comparatively recently. Yes, there were Grands Prix in the 1920s and '30s, and indeed Aston Martins appeared in a number of them. The first was the 1922 French Grand Prix, when it fielded two specially built cars commissioned by wealthy young motor racing driver Count Louis Zborowski.

TT1 and TT2 were so named because they were originally intended for the 1922 Isle of Man TT (Tourist Trophy), but a delay saw them instead make the marque's international racing debut at the French Grand Prix on 15 July 1922, with Zborowski piloting TT1, affectionately nicknamed Green Pea (a car that still exists today).

But these early GPs were not as we know them today. Formula 1 and the world championship were post-war inventions, with the inaugural season in 1950 bringing a whole new level of glamour and prestige to those taking part.

It was not until 1956 that Aston Martin gave serious thought to building a Formula 1 Grand Prix car, conceived as a parallel project with the DBR1. The single-seater DBR4 followed the DBR1's specification very closely with a spaceframe chassis, double wishbone front suspension, a De Dion rear axle and Girling disc brakes.

Those who drove it said it handled well. It seemed that, at pretty much the first time of asking, Aston Martin had produced a Grand Prix car that would be highly competitive at the top level in 1958. Only problem was, it did not race in 1958.

Team manager John Wyer later described the decision to delay the debut of the DBR4 by a year as 'fatal'. The reasons were entirely understandable: the company had been trying since 1952 to win the World Sportscar Championship and

ABOVE: The DBR4 was Aston Martin's first Formula 1 contender, but by the time it made its debut in 1959 its front-engined design was no match for the nimble new breed of mid-engined cars.

the DBR1 really did seem to be in with a shot in 1958, so all resources were piled into that.

But in the very first race of the 1958 Formula 1 season, something happened that had never occurred before: a mid-engined car won. Next time out, it happened again. By 1959 everyone – with the possible exception of Ferrari – could see that the cart-before-the-horse design was the future. In sitting out the single greatest transitional season in F1 history, the DBR4 effectively ruled itself out of contention.

That said, when it made its race debut with Roy Salvadori driving at the International Trophy Race at Silverstone on 2 May 1959, it broke the lap record and came second only to Jack Brabham's Cooper, a combination that would go on to collect the F1 drivers' title later that year. It seemed too good to be true, and so it proved, for the DBR4 had already achieved the best result of its life.

The rest of the season produced a mere handful of top ten results as the DBR4 struggled and failed to match either the handling of the mid-engined Coopers or the power of the front-engined Ferraris. It would be almost 60 years before Aston Martin would take up the F1 challenge again.

The first signs that it had fresh designs on F1 came with the Valkyrie hypercar project, which saw the company form a technical partnership with Red Bull Racing and its technical director Adrian Newey. As part of the deal, the Aston Martin name appeared on the grid in 2018 as title sponsor for the Red Bull team.

Then for 2021 came a full return to F1 with a rebranding of the Racing Point team, which happened to be owned by a consortium led by AML executive chairman Lawrence Stroll. It was all part of Stroll's masterplan to propel Aston Martin into the highest echelons of motorsport and to use success therein to boost sales and stock value.

As statements of intent go, signing four-times World Champion Sebastian Vettel was as serious as it gets. Alongside

BELOW: Aston Martin made a full return to F1 in 2021 with a rebranding of what had been the Racing Point team (previously Force India). Its first car was this, the AMR21.

FERRARI

him was Stroll's son, Lance, who despite being just 22 years old was entering his fifth season of F1 and blessed with genuine talent. The good-looking AMR21 race car would use customer Mercedes engines, and work would soon begin on an impressive new 400,000sq ft (37,160sq m) headquarters a stone's throw from the Silverstone GP circuit to house the 800-strong workforce.

Vettel claimed the new team's first podium in the 2021 Azerbaijan GP and there would be further glimmers of potential in both the 2021 and 2022 seasons without Aston Martin ever quite setting the F1 world alight. But that was all about to change.

For 2023 the budget cap for all teams dropped to $135m, which in theory meant a level playing field in terms of resources with the likes of Mercedes, Red Bull and Ferrari. The other big news was the retirement of Vettel and the hiring of two-time champion Fernando Alonso as his replacement. Despite his more mature years (he celebrated his forty-second birthday during the course of the season) Alonso quickly showed he had lost none of his speed or race-craft with a string of podiums and both drivers placing consistently in the points. Alonso finished fourth in the drivers' standings with 206 points and no fewer than eight podiums. The team's final points tally was 280, putting them fifth in the constructors' championship, 160 points ahead of Alpine-Renault in sixth place. It had been a season to remember.

There was more good news when it was announced that from 2026 Aston Martin F1 would have Honda as its engine supplier with full factory support, including bespoke power units designed specifically for the Aston chassis. Works team status is often seen as a fundamental ingredient to becoming a genuine title contender. Aston Martin's growing army of fans were certainly hoping so.

OPPOSITE: Aston Martin F1 made its ambitions clear when it signed four-time champion Sebastian Vettel, and Vettel repaid them with a first podium at Azerbaijan.

crypto.com
ARCTOS
aramco

BELOW: A string of podium finishes in 2023 confirmed Aston Martin's arrival in the uppermost echelon of motorsport.

# THE
# 007 ASTONS

# AN UNBREAKABLE BOND

From the DB5 in *Goldfinger* to the Valhalla concept car in *No Time to Die*, no other marque is as tightly entwined with the Bond legend as Aston Martin. But then no other car echoes the suave sophistication and effortless cool of 007 quite like an Aston.

It is quite an image: Sean Connery as James Bond, leaning casually on his Aston Martin DB5 somewhere high in the Swiss Alps. The glamour, the danger, the timeless cool of early Bond are woven tightly into the Aston Martin DNA, and it is all encapsulated right there in a single frame.

This press shot was one of a number used to publicize *Goldfinger* on its cinema release in the autumn of 1964. It was taken by an uncredited stills photographer in a break during filming on the Furka Pass, and it showed Connery's Bond and Aston's DB5 to be perfectly matched.

The combination was one of several factors that helped to make Goldfinger — the third cinematic outing for 007, but the first for the DB5 — such a global hit and the Bond franchise a cultural phenomenon.

OPPOSITE: Two icons, Bond and DB5, caught in a single frame.

BELOW: One of the original 1960s Bond DB5s on the Furka Pass in Switzerland, where the famous chase scenes were shot for 1964's *Goldfinger*.

Connery's 007 had previously been seen driving a Sunbeam Alpine in *Dr No* and canoodling in a pre-war Bentley drophead in *From Russia With Love*, a nod to the fact that he drove a Bentley in several of the Fleming novels. But just as in the books, he would swap the Bentley for an Aston (a DB MkIII in the books, the then-new DB5 when *Goldfinger* filming began).

In the film, our first glimpse of his new company car comes – where else – in the workshops of Q Branch. "*Where's my Bentley*?" Bond asks Q. "*Oh, it's had its day, I'm afraid*," comes the reply. "*Well, it's never let me down*," murmurs Bond. "*M's orders, 007. You'll be using this Aston Martin DB5 with modifications. Now pay attention please…*"

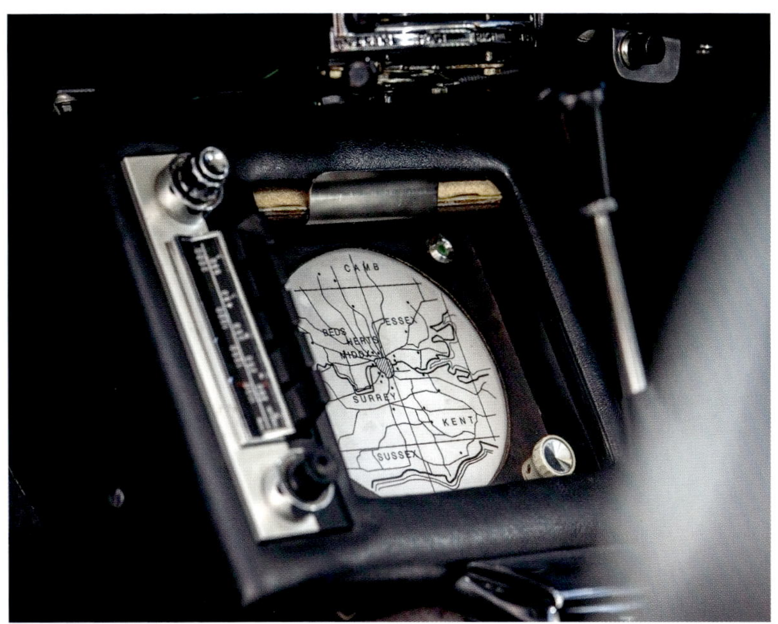


ABOVE: The DB5's celebrated gadgets included a radar screen concealed in the centre console; others included the bulletproof shield and, most famously of all, the ejector seat.

Hard to believe now, but Aston Martin was initially reluctant to supply a car to EON Productions. Fortunately, it eventually relented and, in January 1964, released a surplus DB5 prototype, then still painted in its original Dubonnet Rosso. Registered BMT 216A, it was kitted out by John Stears of EON with production designer Ken Adam's famous gadgets and outshopped as the Effects Car with the now famous Silver Birch paintjob. Soon after, Aston also loaned EON a standard production-spec DB5 for the regular driving scenes, to this day still known as the Road Car.

The film and the car were both such a hit that the DB5 was deployed again for *Thunderball* and a further two cars were subsequently kitted out with all the gadgets for promotional duties. When Corgi produced its famous model, complete with ejector seat and blue overall-clad baddie, schoolboys everywhere wanted the new must-have toy. A legend had been born.

Bond had a dalliance with a Toyota 2000 GT (a one-off open-top version because Connery was too big to get comfortable in the coupé) in *You Only Live Twice*, but he was back in an Aston – the then-new DBS – for 1968's *On Her Majesty's Secret Service*, though that was with the Australian actor George Lazenby at the wheel.

Aston Martin was asked to loan two examples of the DBS for filming. Unlike the tricked-up DB5, the Vantage-spec DBS was pretty much factory-standard, with the exception of a glovebox-mounted rifle. Both film and car were long regarded as less successful examples of their type, but *On Her Majesty's Secret Service* is now considered one of the best Bonds and the DBS very much a desirable Aston Martin.

Connery returned for 1971's *Diamonds are Forever*, and while the star car was a Mustang, there was a fleeting glimpse of a DBS V8 in the Q lab being equipped with missiles. Alas, we never got to see that particular pairing.

For various contractual reasons, it was almost 20 years before EON renewed Bond's association with Aston Martin for 1987's *The Living Daylight*s. At the start of the film we see our hero, played for the first time by Timothy Dalton, driving a V8 Volante with Cumberland Grey coachwork and upholstered in black leather. This car was in fact the personal transport of Victor Gauntlett, chairman of AML at the time. Indeed Gauntlett was offered – and nearly accepted – a role as a KGB colonel in the film, but was too busy saving the company to take the time off.

In the film the Volante is 'winterized' in Q's workshop, ostensibly through the addition of a hardtop. In reality the car was switched for a regular AM V8 saloon, the producers procuring three well-used examples for stunt work, while seven fibreglass replicas were also used, some of which have survived. Chassis number V8SOR 12070, complete with detachable skis, was retained by EON and has been seen on display in the touring *Bond in Motion* exhibition.

For the twentieth film in the series, 2002's *Die Another Day*, Pierce Brosnan's 007 was given the then-brand-new V12 Vanquish, finished in Tungsten Silver with Charcoal leather to echo the colour combo of the *Goldfinger* DB5. Behind the scenes, four special effects cars had to be fitted with a four-wheel-drive system for the action sequences shot on a frozen lake in Iceland, so the 5.9-litre V12s were replaced with 300bhp Ford Boss 302 V8s mounted as far back in the chassis

BELOW: Complete with skis, the V8 saloon from 1987's *The Living Daylights*, which saw Timothy Dalton put on Bond's tuxedo for the first of two outings.

ABOVE: Filming 2008's *Quantum of Solace*, which starred Daniel Craig as 007. Here Bond's latest company car, a DBS, is looking rather the worse for wear.

as possible. This allowed sufficient room for the fitment of a front differential and driveshafts, plus space for weaponry behind the grille. An interesting feature of the 4wd Vanquish was the automatic gearbox that allowed for 120mph (193km/h) in both forward and reverse!

The DB5 returned for 1995's *GoldenEye*, with three further original DB5s being refurbished for use in the film. One of the three, chassis number DB5/1484/R, is actually still owned by EON and went on to star in *Tomorrow Never Dies*, *Skyfall* and *Spectre*.

It was back to another brand-new model, this time the DB9-based DBS, for Daniel Craig's first outing as 007 in 2006's *Casino Royale*. On screen, the DBS famously meets its demise in a spectacular barrel-roll. The first stunt car refused to co-operate, so the second was installed with a nitrogen-powered ram to punch the tarmac at the correct moment to start the car rolling.

Bond was back in the DBS for 2008's *Quantum of Solace*. This time ten brand-new DBSs were supplied, the first four for special effects, the remainder as 'hero' cars for close-ups, interior shots and promotional work. It was the first time actual production cars had been supplied for special effects in the full knowledge that they would be trashed during filming. Two of these were lost during production, one when it plunged into Lake Garda in a freak accident that the driver was fortunate to survive.

Cinema audiences around the world cheered when Bond pulled open the doors of his lock-up to reveal his beloved DB5 (immaculately preserved) in *Skyfall*. Later we got to see the classic Aston in full flight, making an overnight dash from central London to the spectacular highlands of Scotland. As well as two actual DB5s, a Porsche 928-based replica and a sophisticated fifth-scale model were also used. These were the vehicles shot to pieces by cannon fire from the baddies's helicopter; Aston fans were mightily relieved to learn that no real DB5s were harmed in the making of this film!

For *Spectre*, Aston Martin went one further and effectively created a new model just for the film. This was the DB10 – originally conceived as a concept car by AML to suggest a future Vantage, but spotted by Bond director Sam Mendes on a tour of the factory. "*That's the car I want in the movie!*", he reportedly exclaimed.

ABOVE: The DB10 that featured in *Spectre* was never offered for sale to the general public – just ten were built, eight for use in filming, the remaining two for promotional duties.

The DB10 was hand-built in a strictly limited batch of just ten cars and never offered for sale. In fact the carbon-fibre skin was all-new, but underneath was a stretched and widened VH-era V8 Vantage. It was even built by a department called Q Advanced Engineering.

Most recently, Bond was back in his DB5 for 2021's much-delayed *No Time to Die*. Or so it appeared. In fact for most of the film's action sequences, audiences were watching artfully created replicas based around the mechanical parts of – whisper it – the early-2000s BMW M3. Using real DB5s for stunts was not an option, so Aston built eight replicas around a bespoke spaceframe chassis, with carbon-fibre bodywork and the M3's naturally aspirated six-cylinder engine standing in for the DB5's own straight-six.

In fact, *No Time to Die* turned into something of an Aston benefit, filmgoers also being treated to the sight of a new DBS Superleggera, a 1980s Vantage and a cameo appearance for the Valhalla concept car.

As the producers recognized, Bond never does it better than when he is behind the wheel of an Aston Martin.

BELOW: Daniel Craig's final appearance as 007 was in 2021's *No Time to Die*. Fans are hoping Bond will be back – and preferably still at the wheel of an Aston.

# INDEX

(Key: *italic* refers to photos/captions)

# CREDITS

The publishers would like to thank the following sources for their kind permission to reproduce the pictures in this book.

ASTON MARTIN HERITAGE TRUST: 12, 13, 20, 29, 49

ASTON MARTIN LAGONDA: 16, 21, 31, 33, 35, 46, 50, 54, 56, 57, 61, 66, 69, 70, 71, 75, 76, 77, 82, 83, 86-87, 89, 90, 91, 93, 94-95, 96, 97, 100, 102-103, 104, 105, 106, 107, 108, 110, 111, 112-113, 115, 119, 120-121, 124, 130, 134, 135, 136, 139, 140, 142-143, 155

DAVID BROWN GROUP: 26

EON: 152

FISKENS: 18-19

GETTY IMAGES: Michael Ochs Archives 146

HOTHOUSE MEDIA: Tim Andrew 15, 40-41, 53; Gus Gregory 39; Matt Howell 84, 92, 126, 138, 151, 154; Justin Leighton 43; James Lipman 55, 58-59; Andy Morgan 64, 67, 68, 72-73, 116, 148, 149; Dean Smith 109; Alex Tapley 80

MOTORSPORT IMAGES: 14; LAT Photographic 128, 129

PRIVATE COLLECTION: 8, 11, 22, 23, 30, 32, 36-37, 42, 52, 131, 133

SHUTTERSTOCK: Sport car hub 4

ROGER STOWERS: 51

R.S. WILLIAMS: 132

ZAGATO: 36 bottom

Every effort has been made to acknowledge correctly and contact the source and/or copyright holder of each picture. Any unintentional errors or omissions will be corrected in future editions of this book.